East of Big Sur
Colorblind Black & White Photography

Decades of being around accomplished artists producing absolutely phenomenal quality work has taught that we are capable of greatness. It is possible to meet our destiny and become it. Experiencing excellence done with such apparent magical ease and humble selfless gratification is the inspiration for this original photography. It is an expression of freedom.

Being colorblind gives an advantage when composing black & white... less confusion. This collection selected from thousands of captures. All images were framed in the camera and presented without edits, genuine as seen through the lens. Panchromatic conversion applied by proprietary process.

Original fine art and custom work available.

info@ BEACHNOISE.com

Joseph Fleming

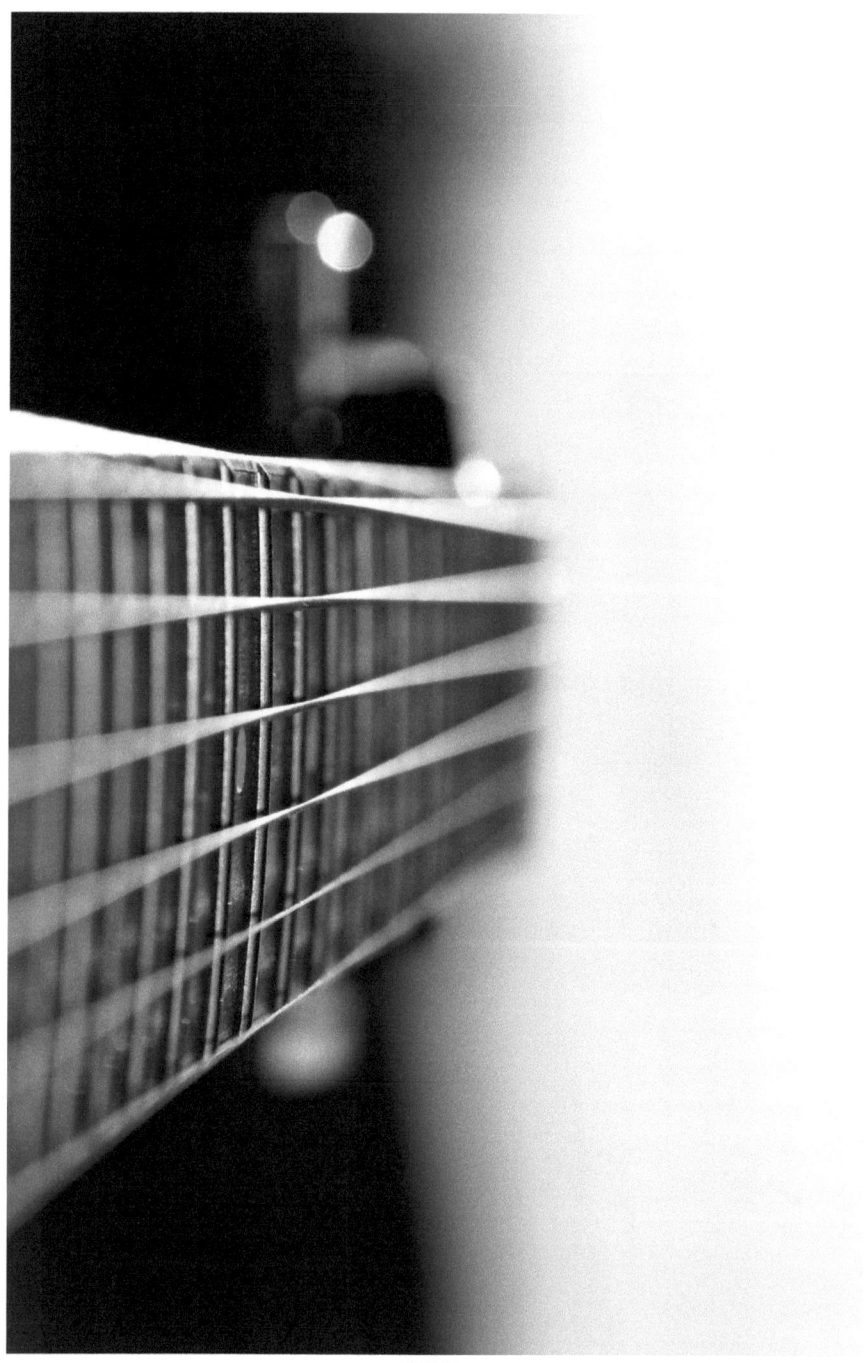

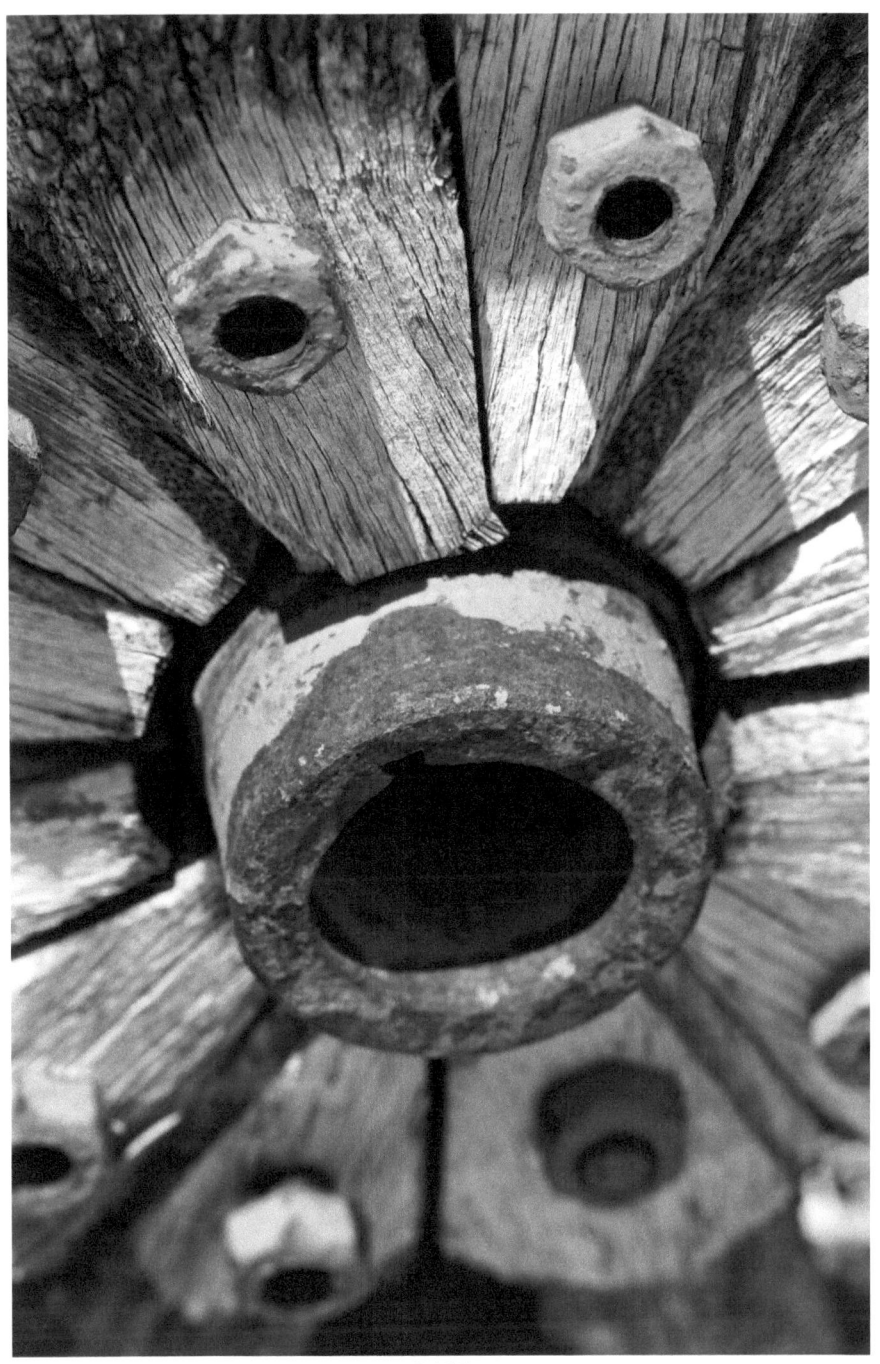

0437

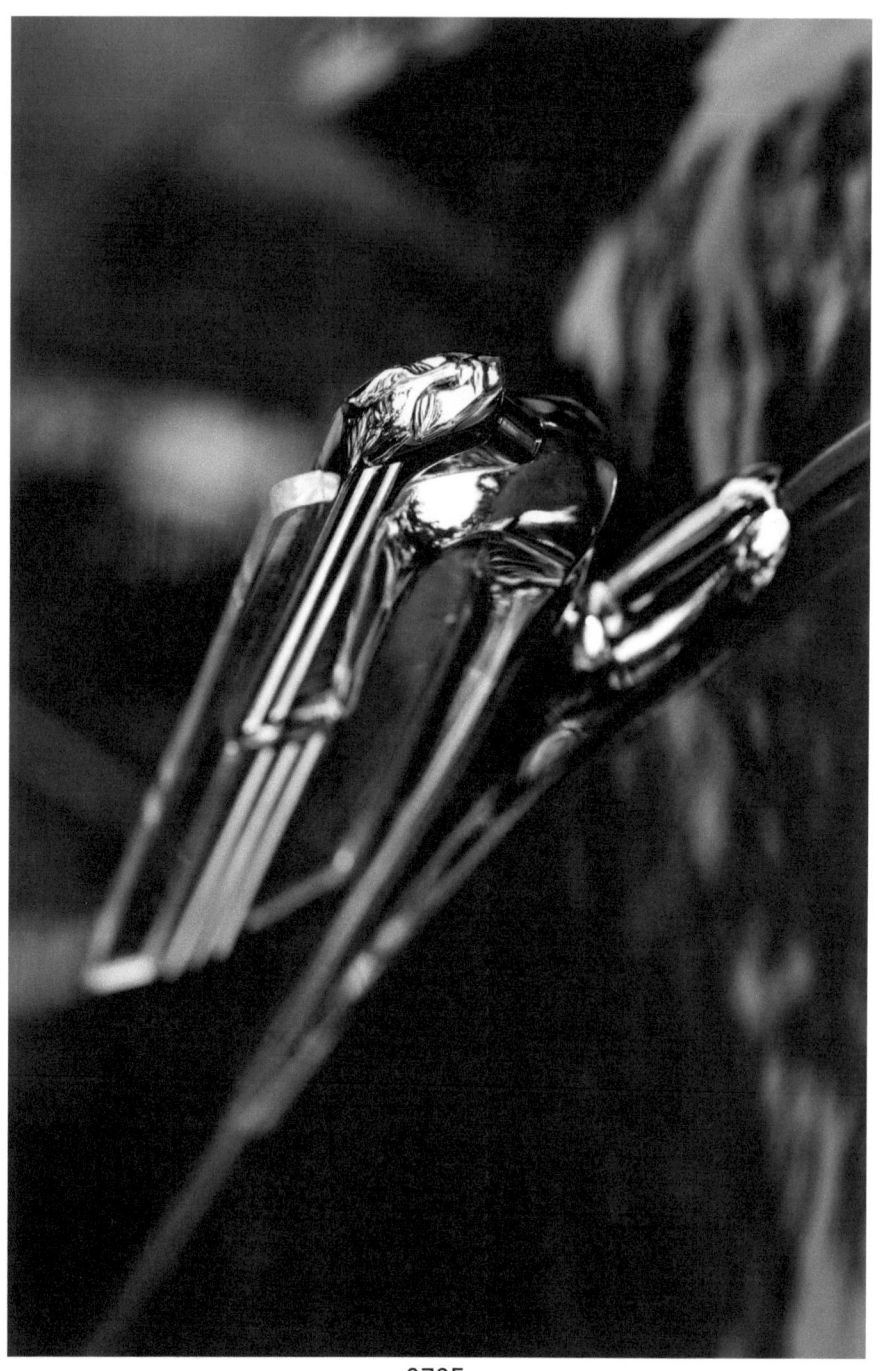

0705

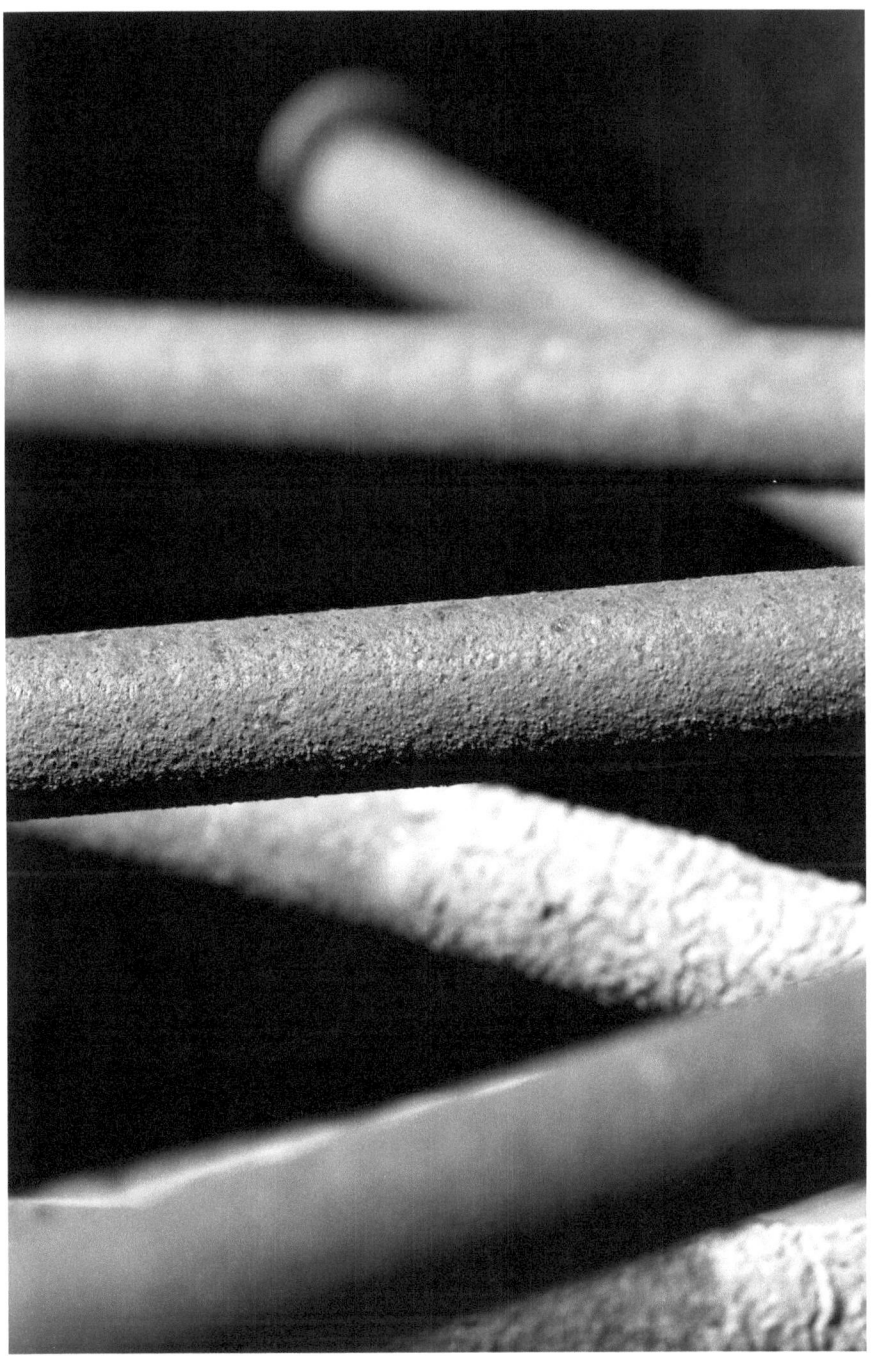

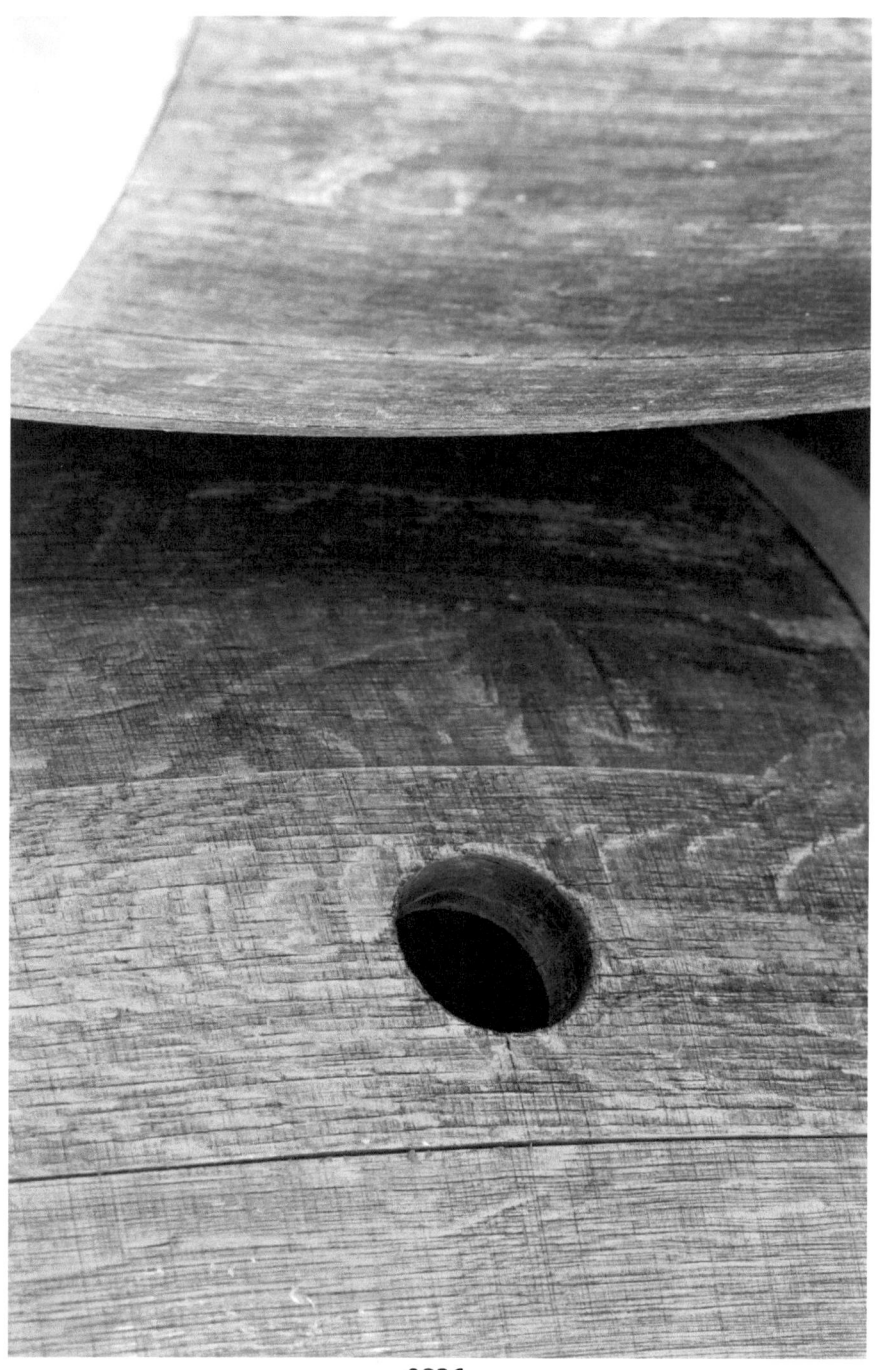

0826

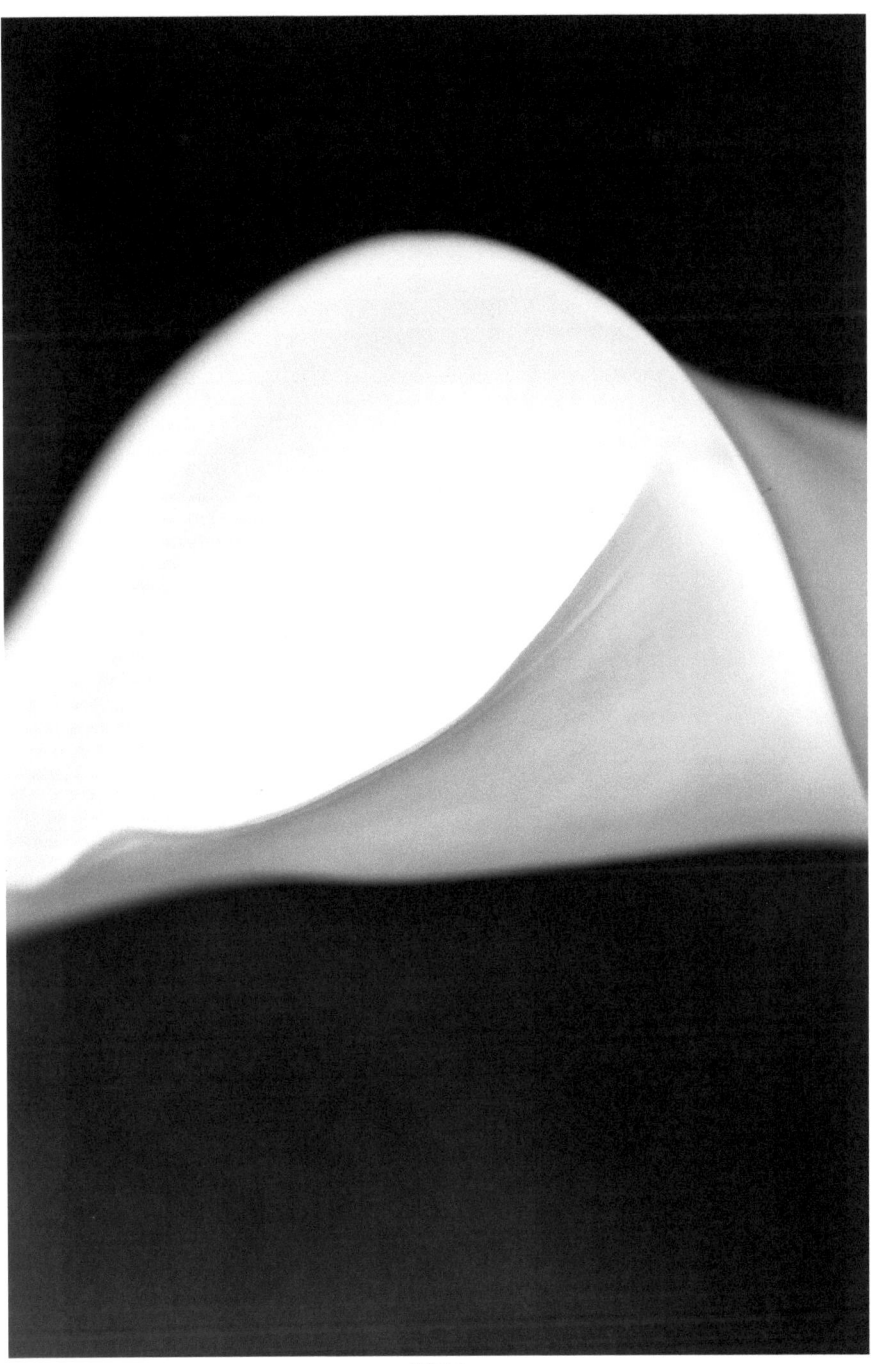

0920

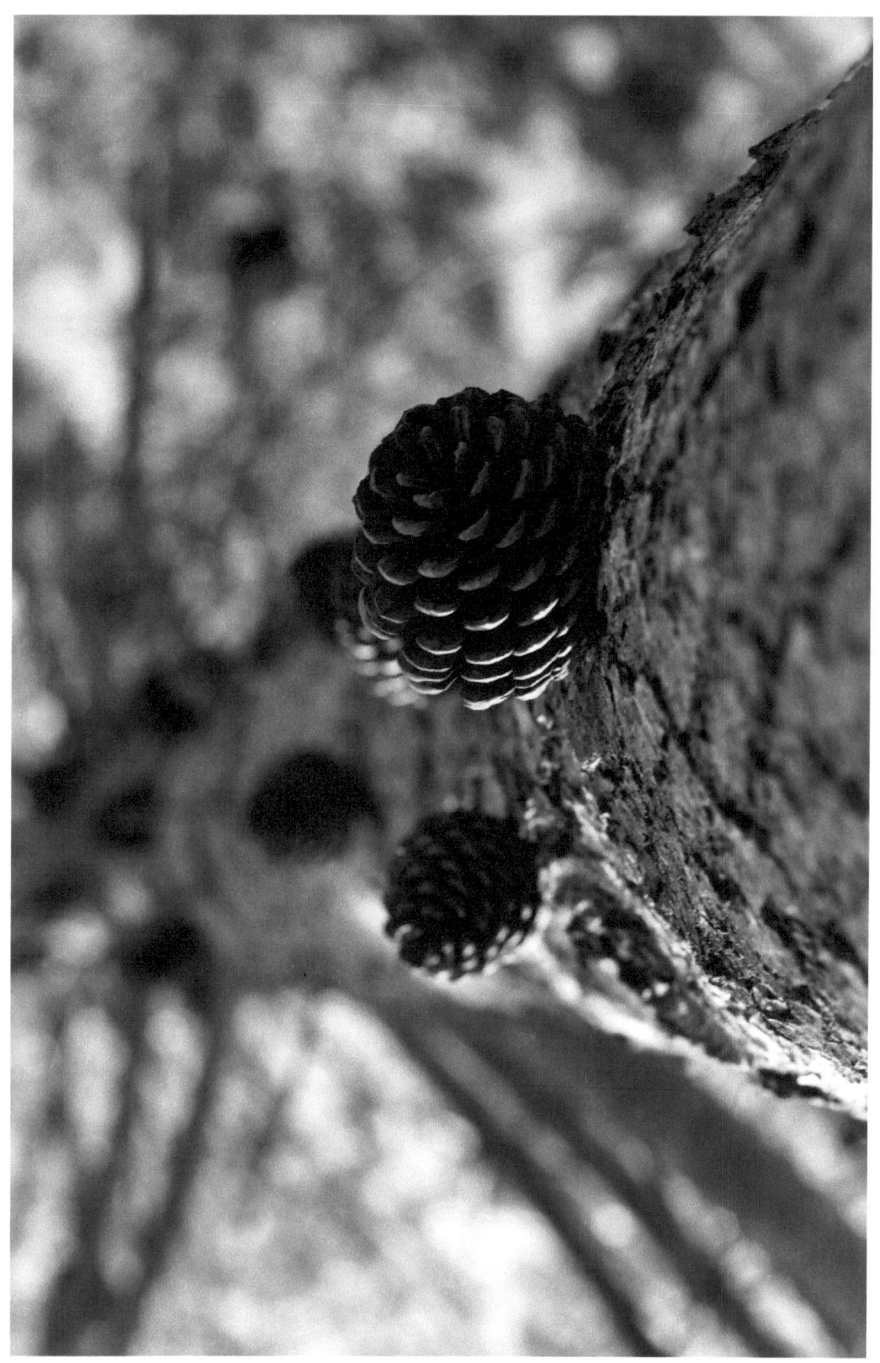

0938

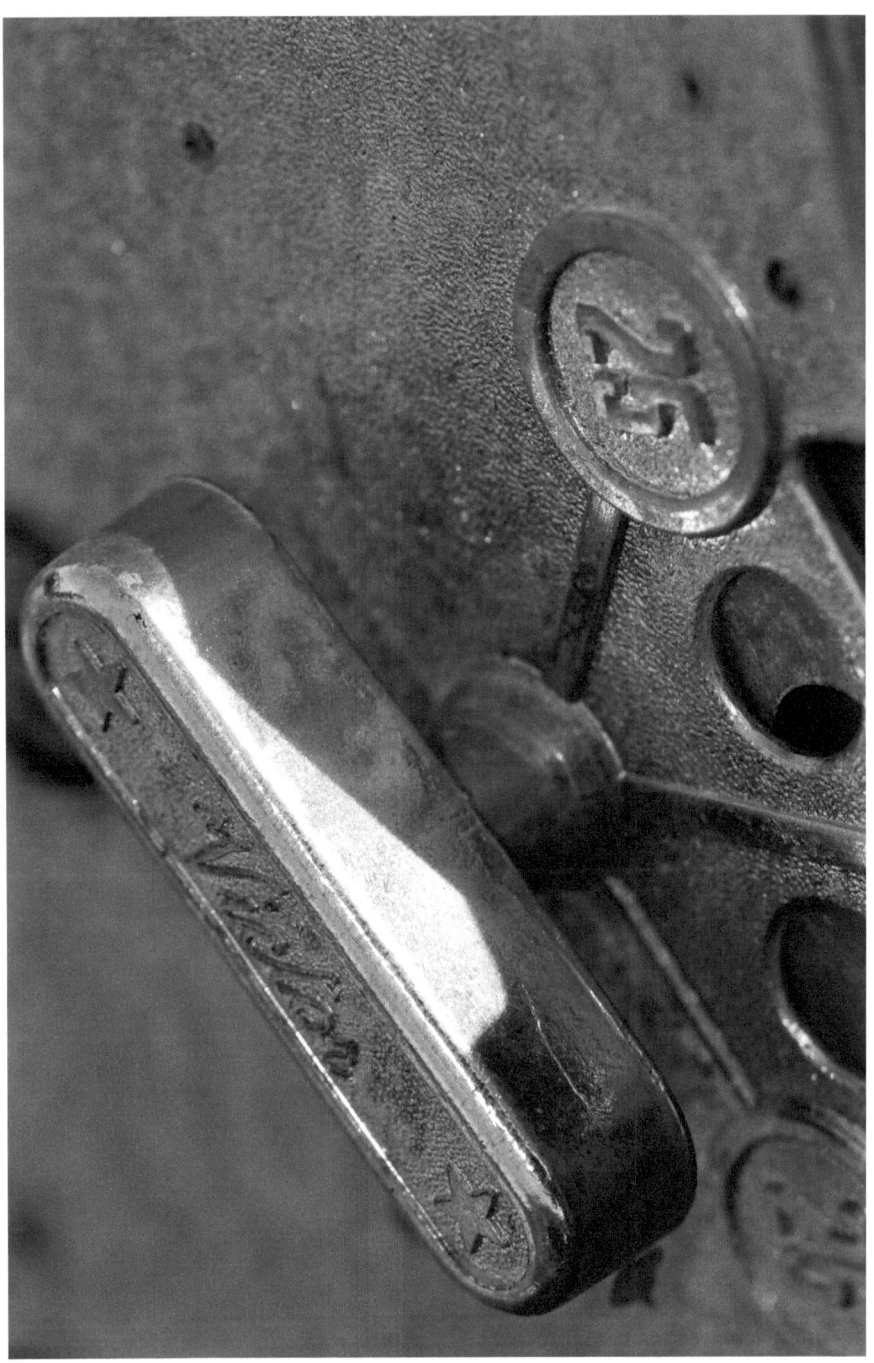

1085

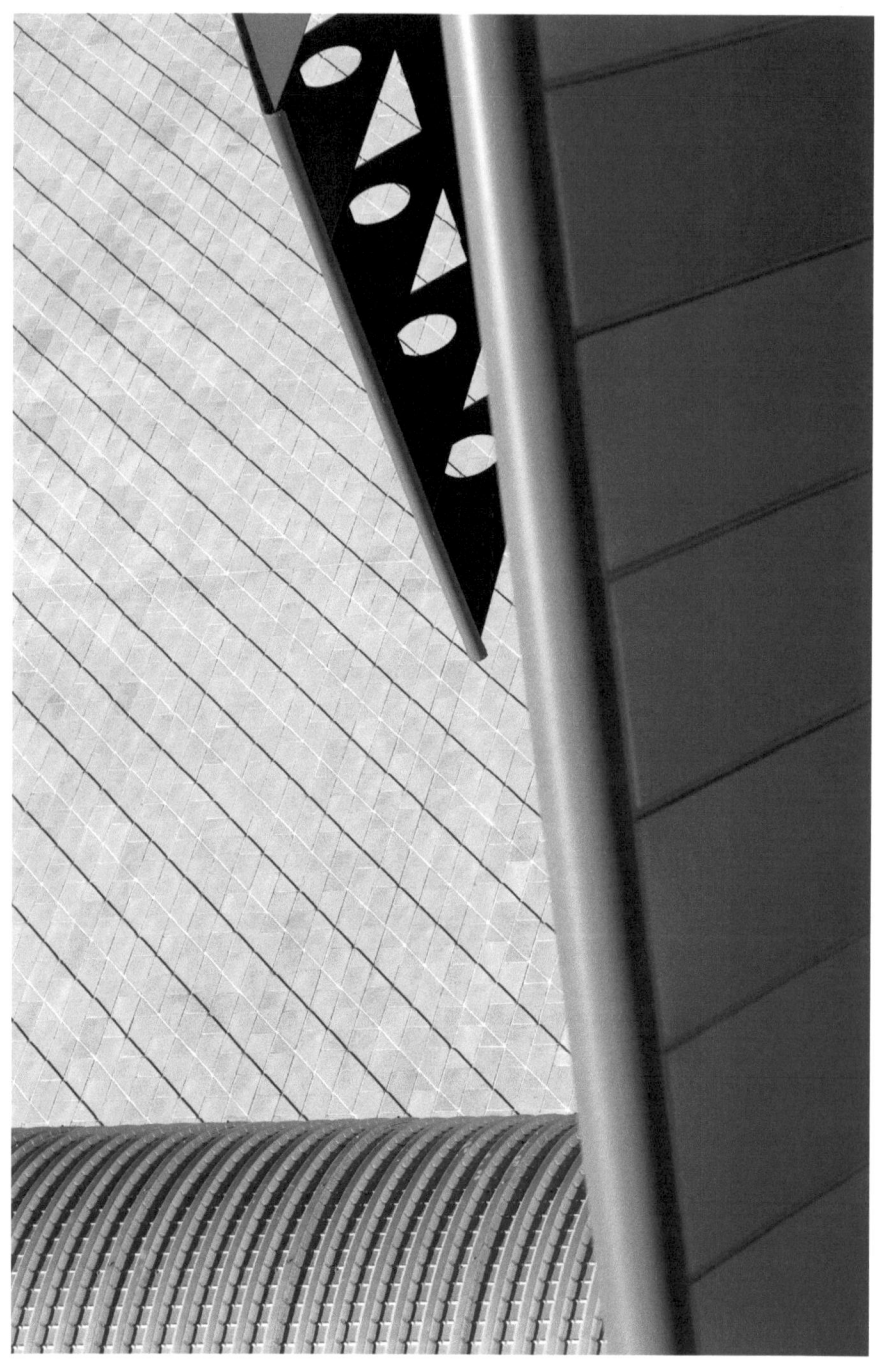

1088

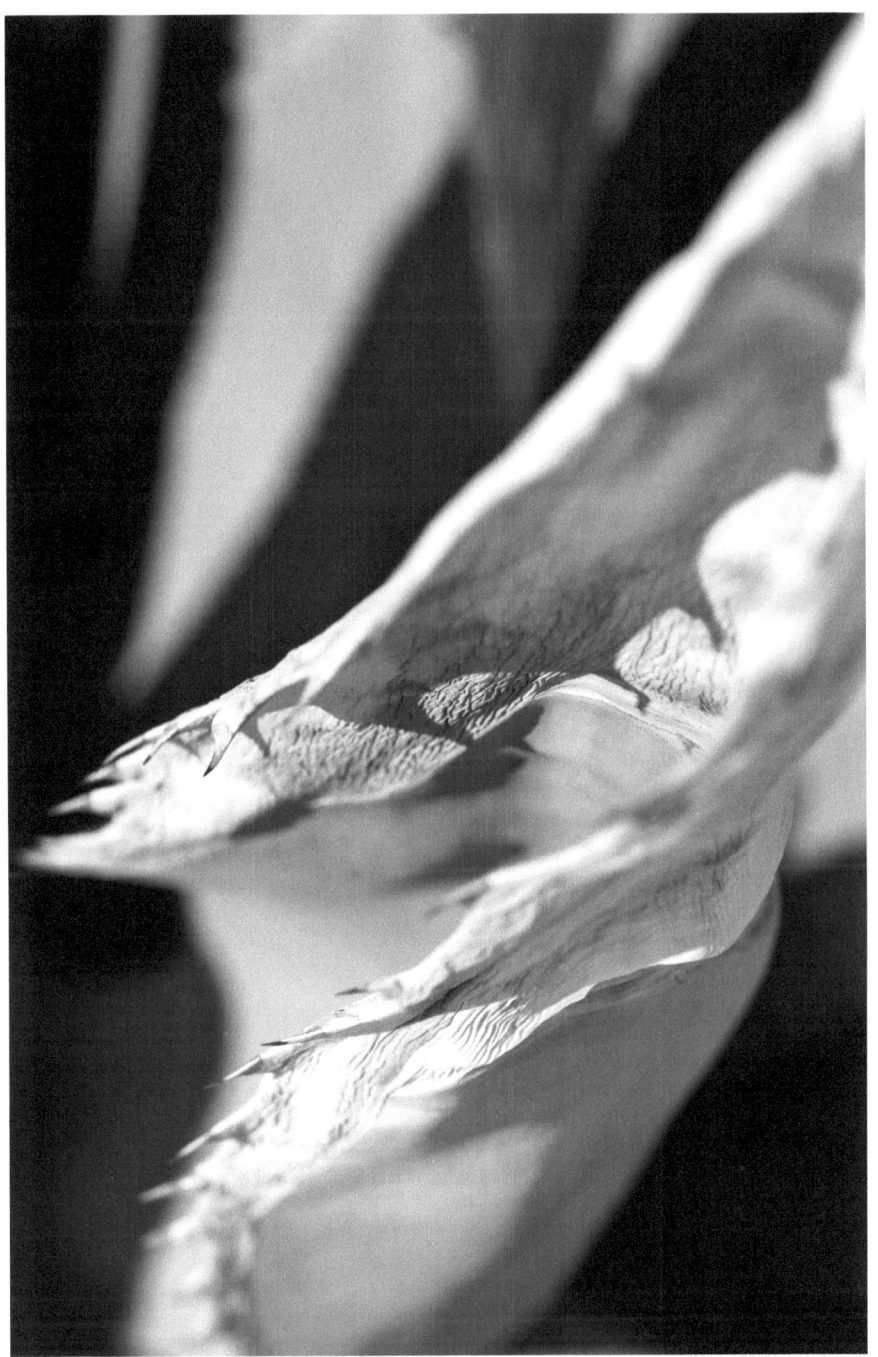

1581

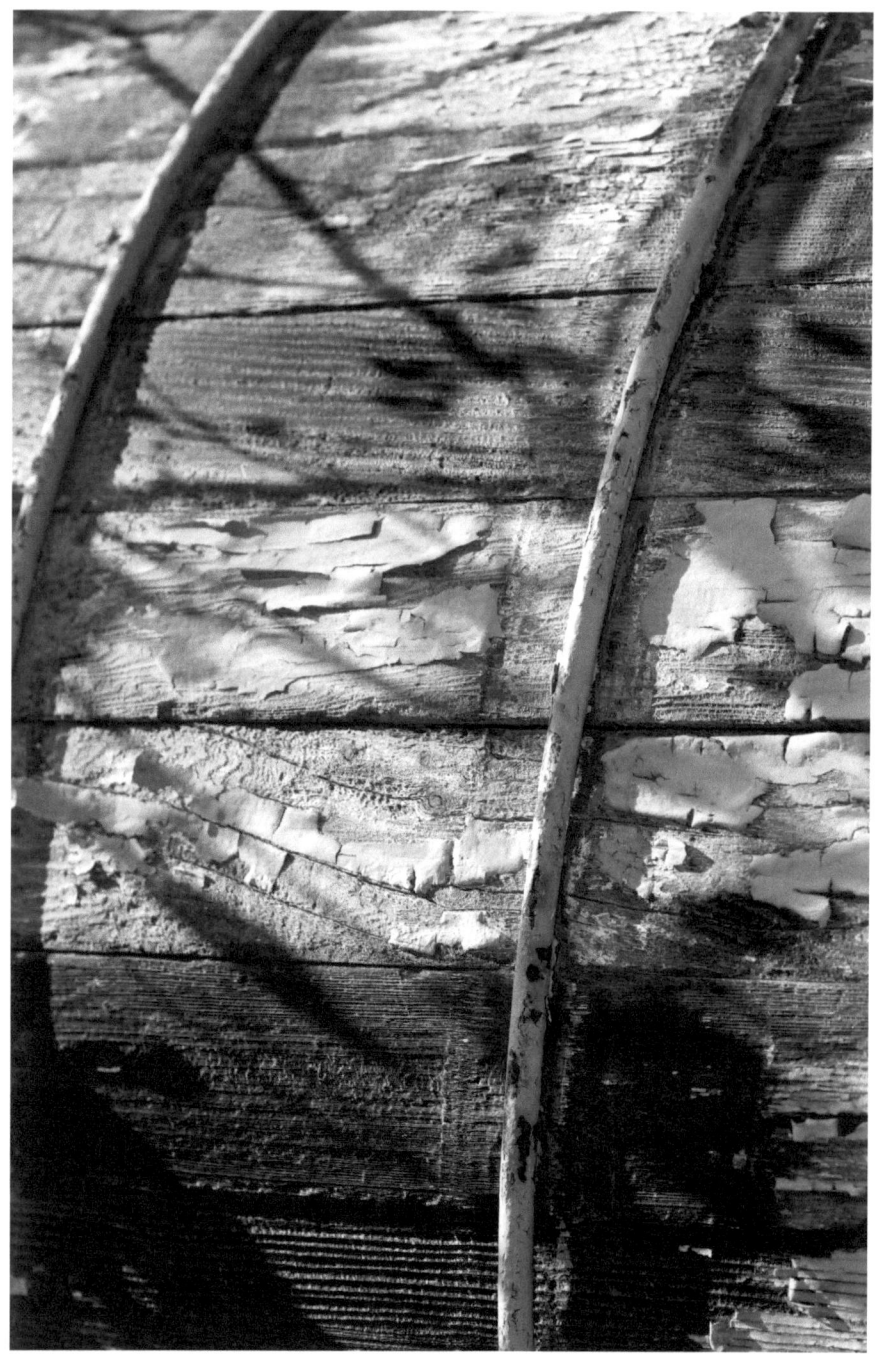

1608

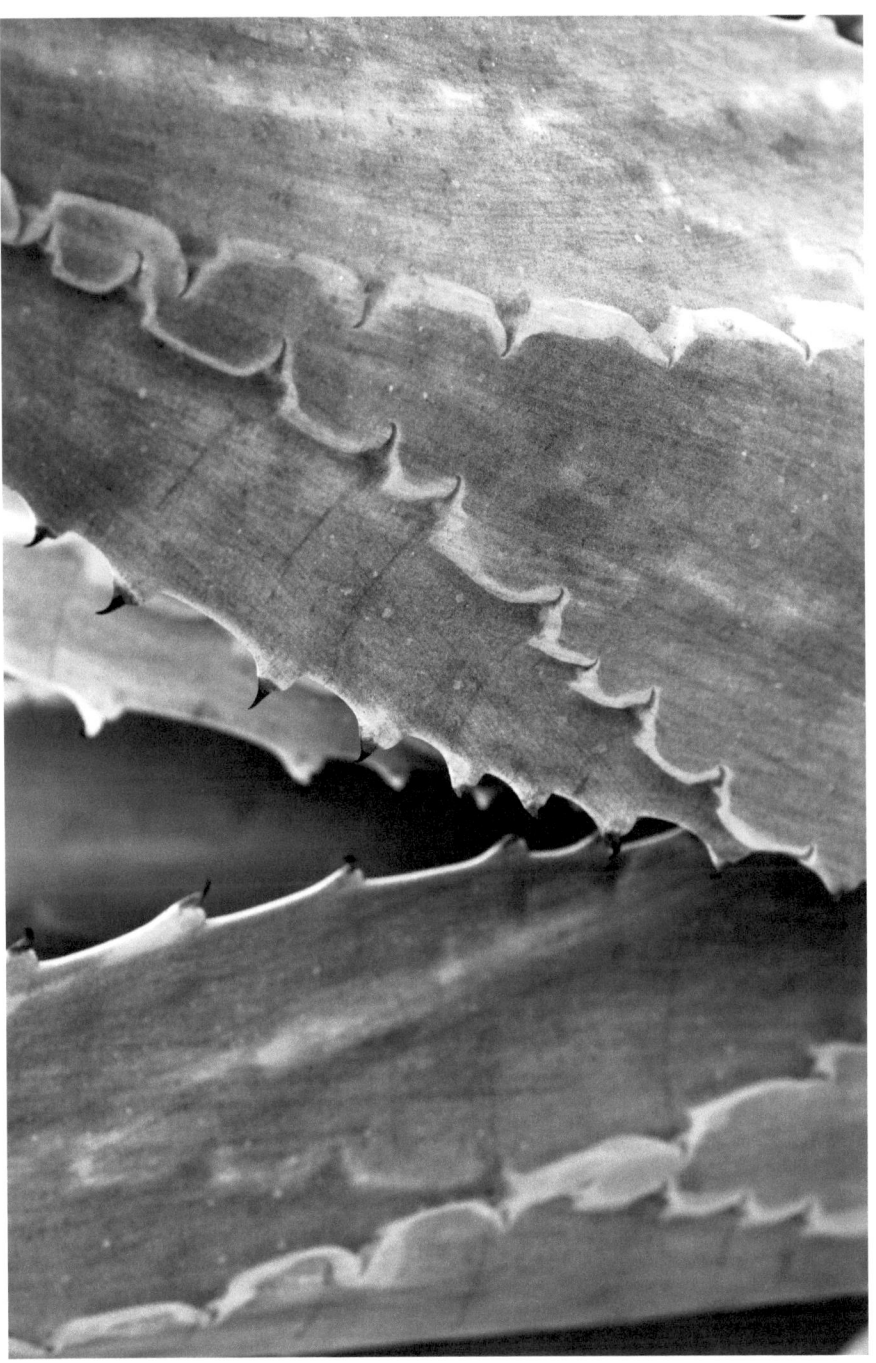

1976

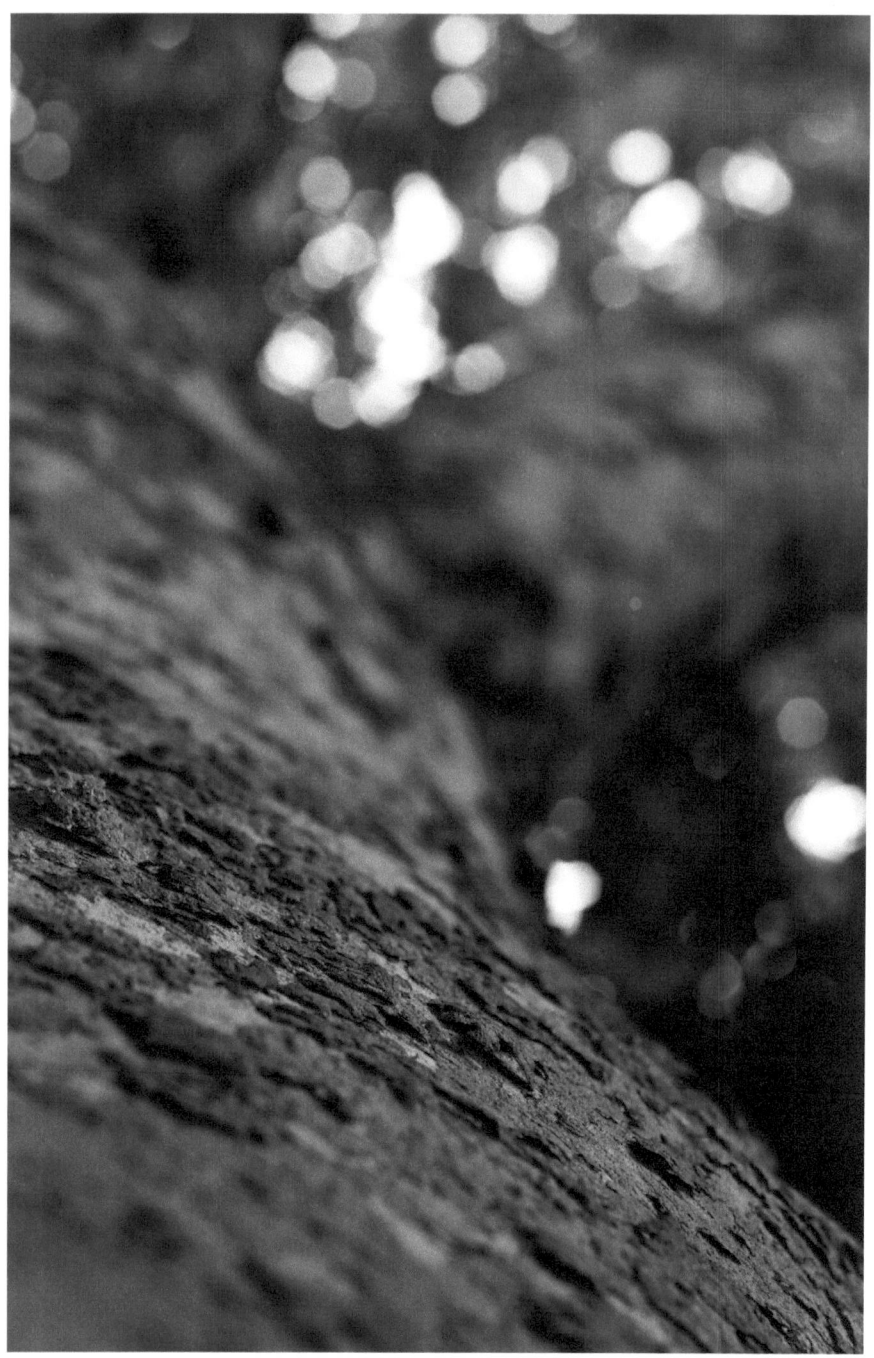

2068

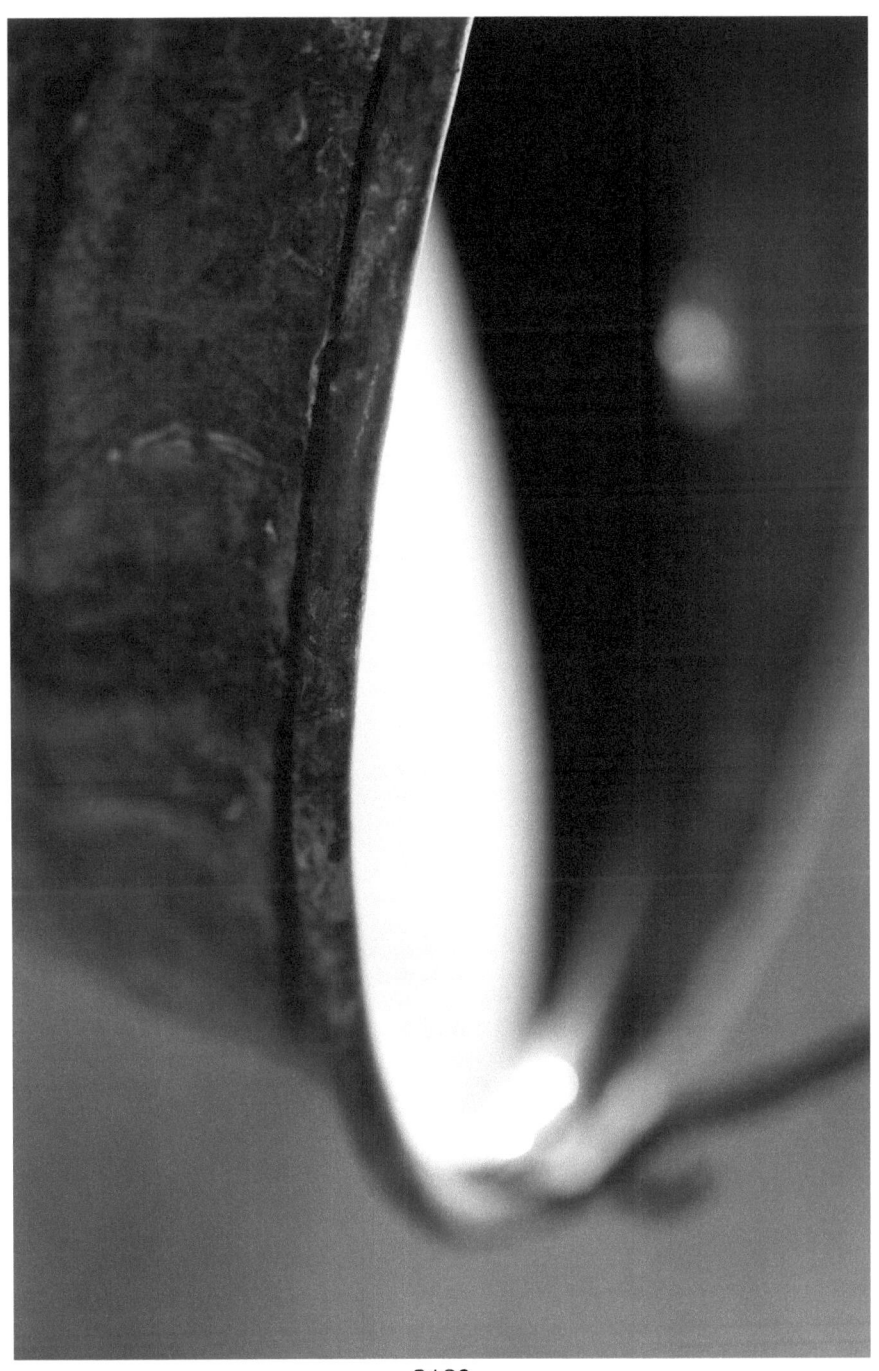

2180

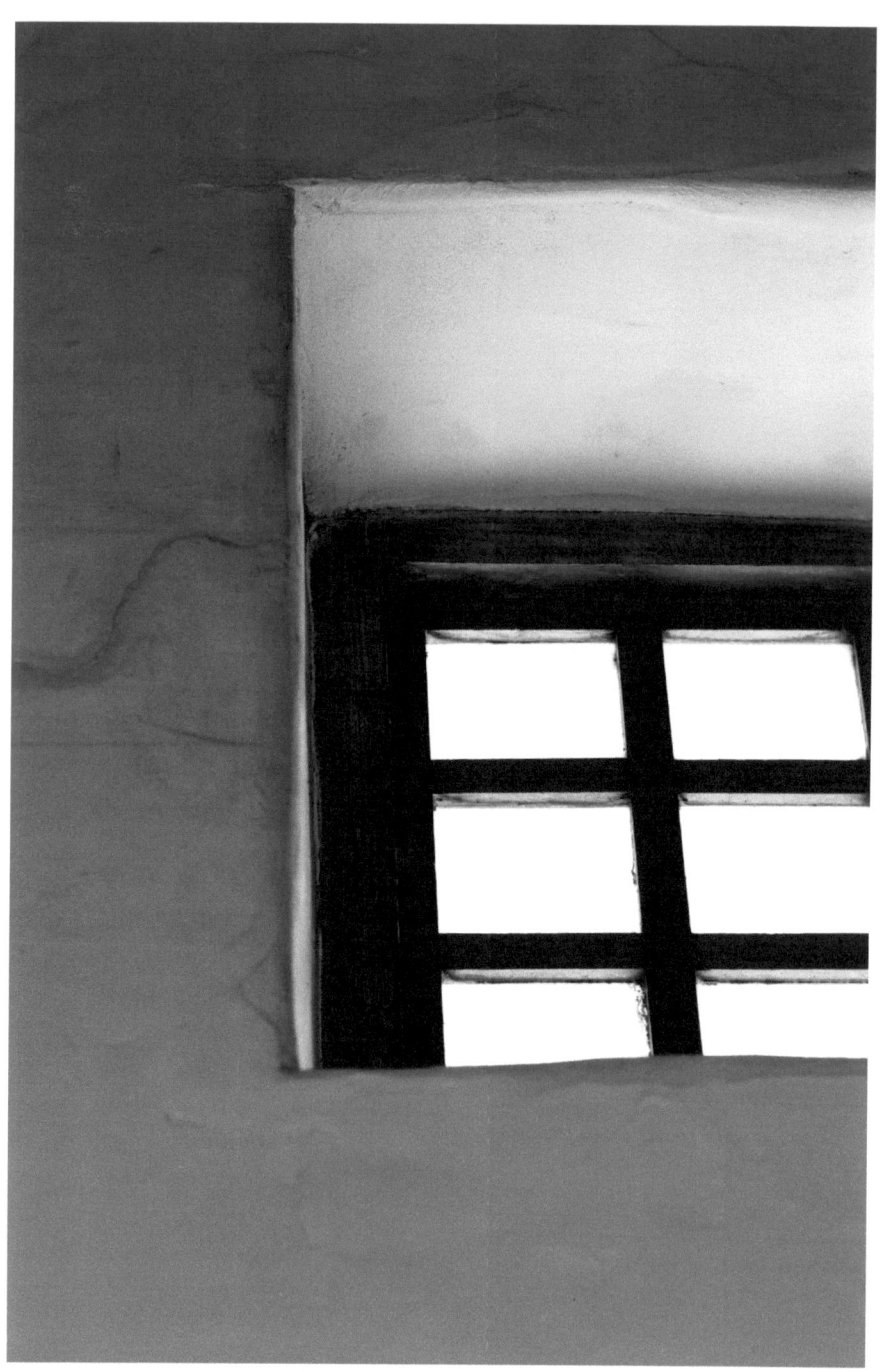

2397

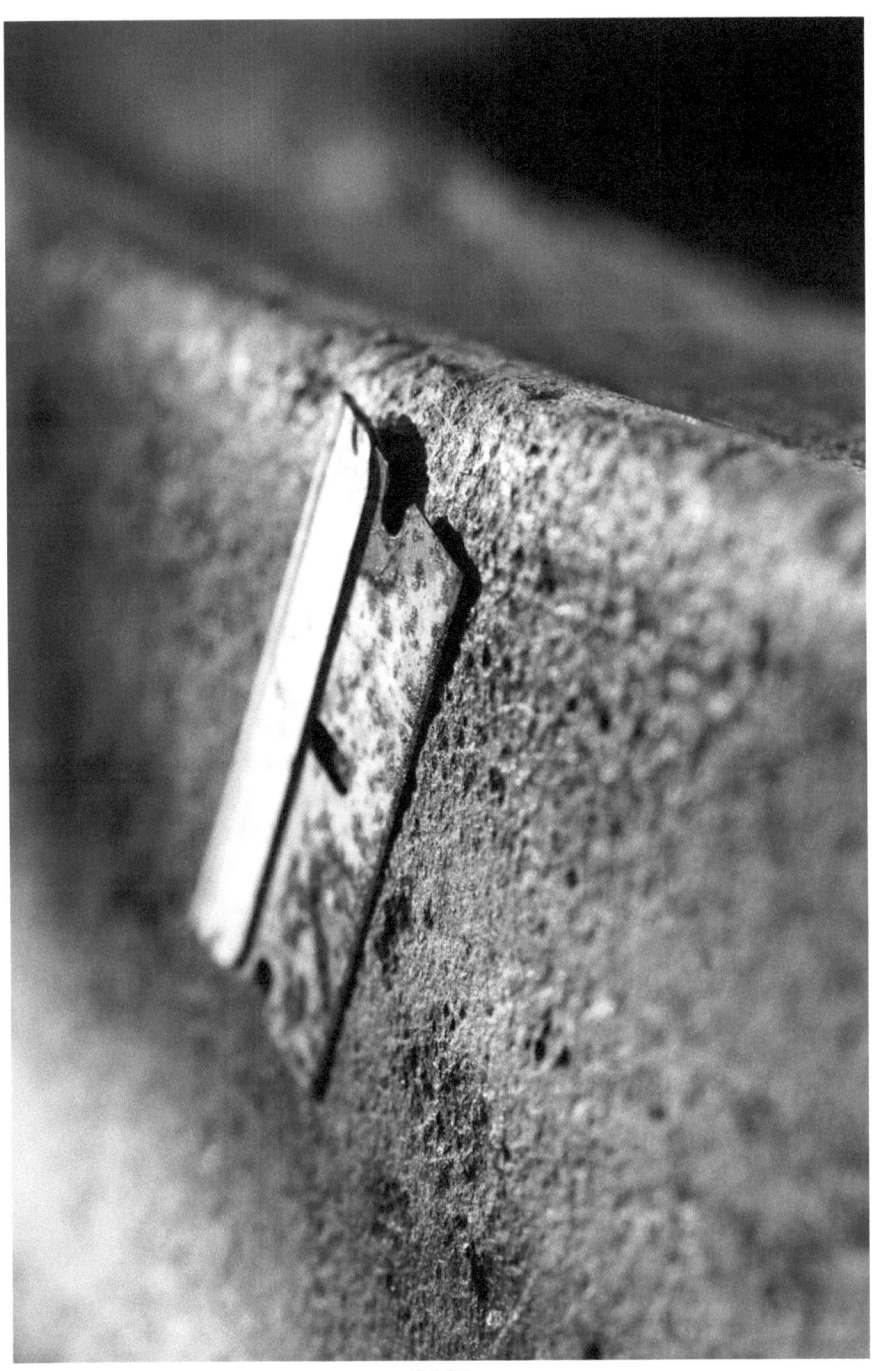

2467

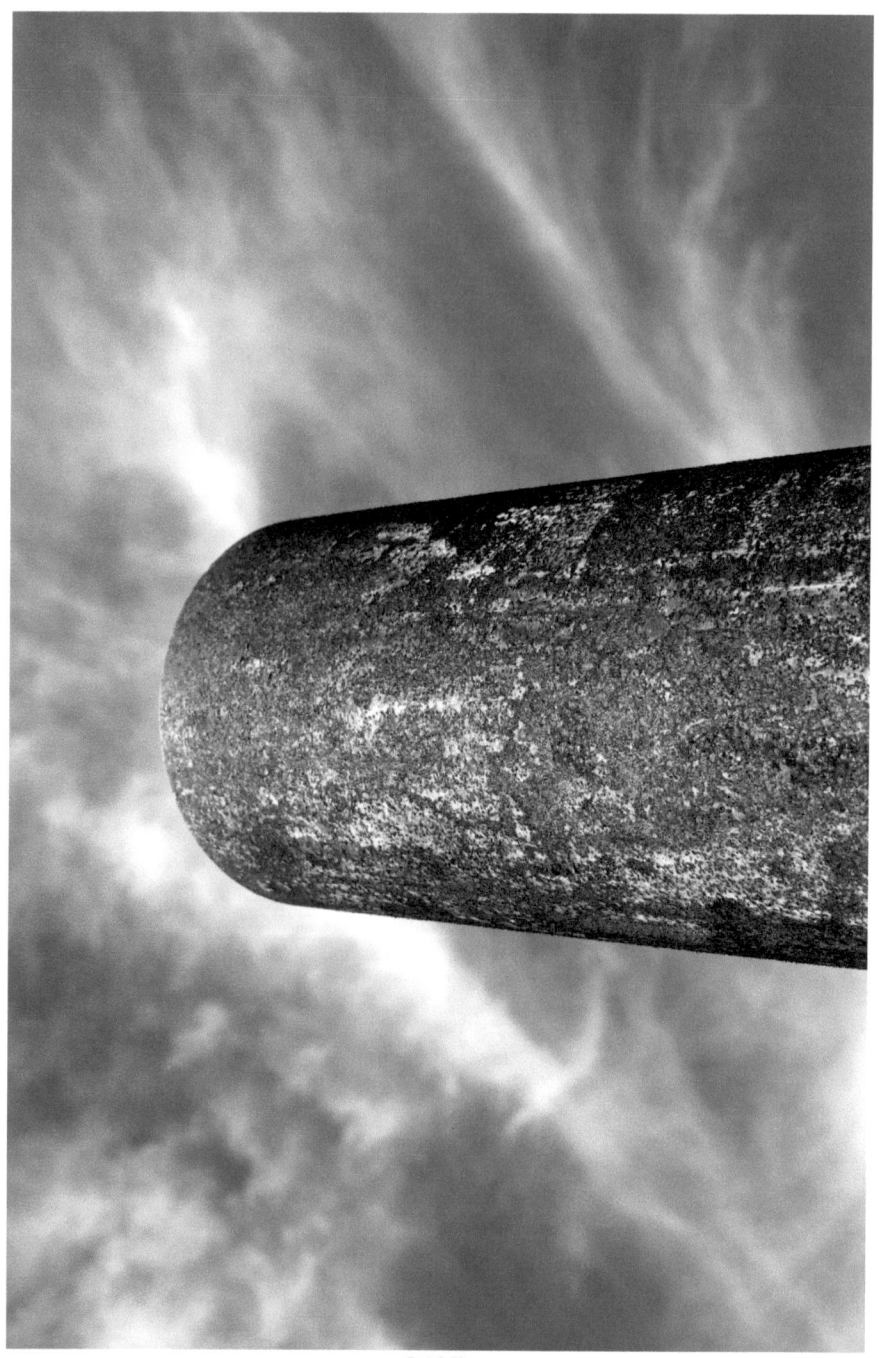

2495

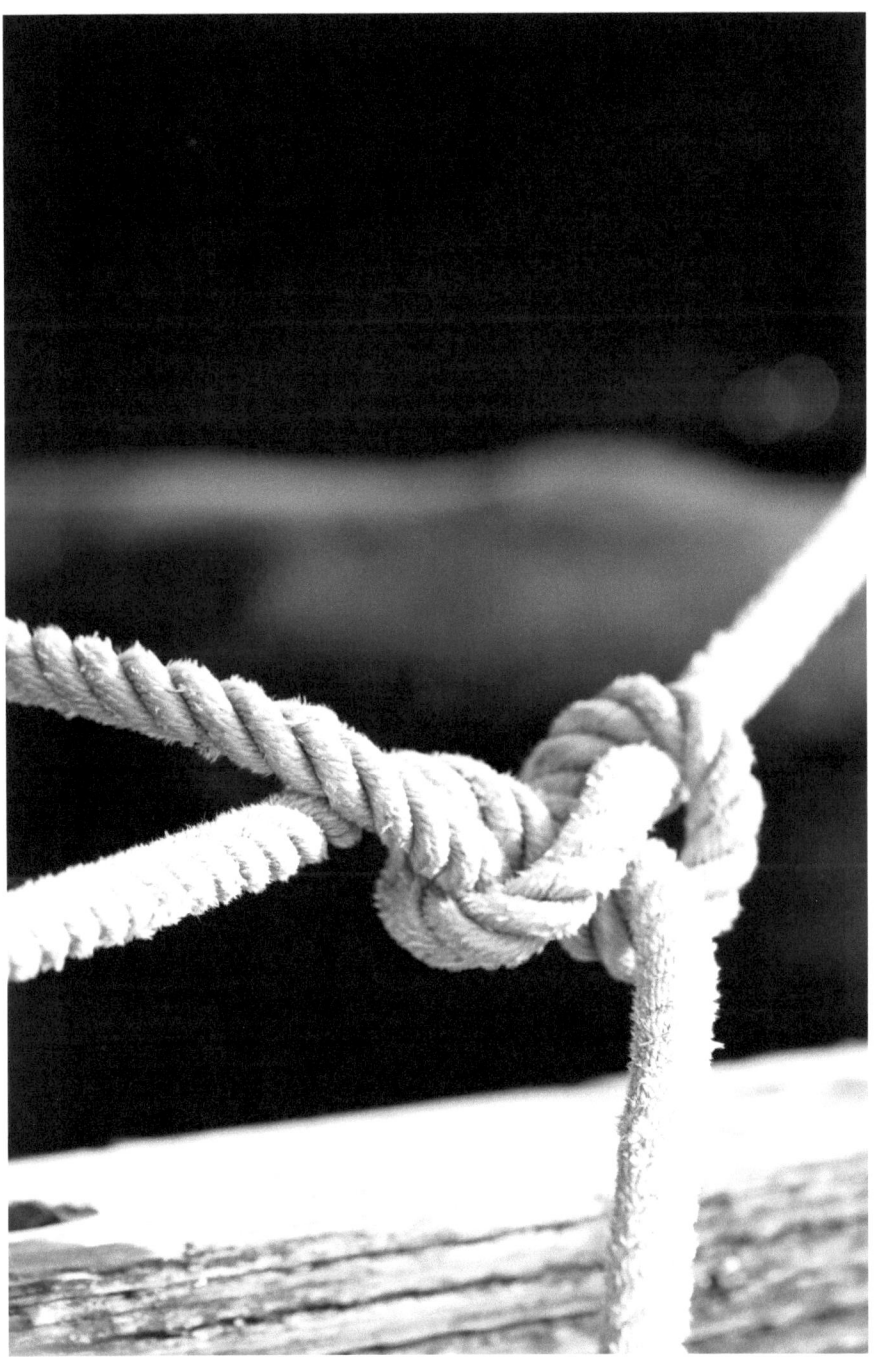

2686

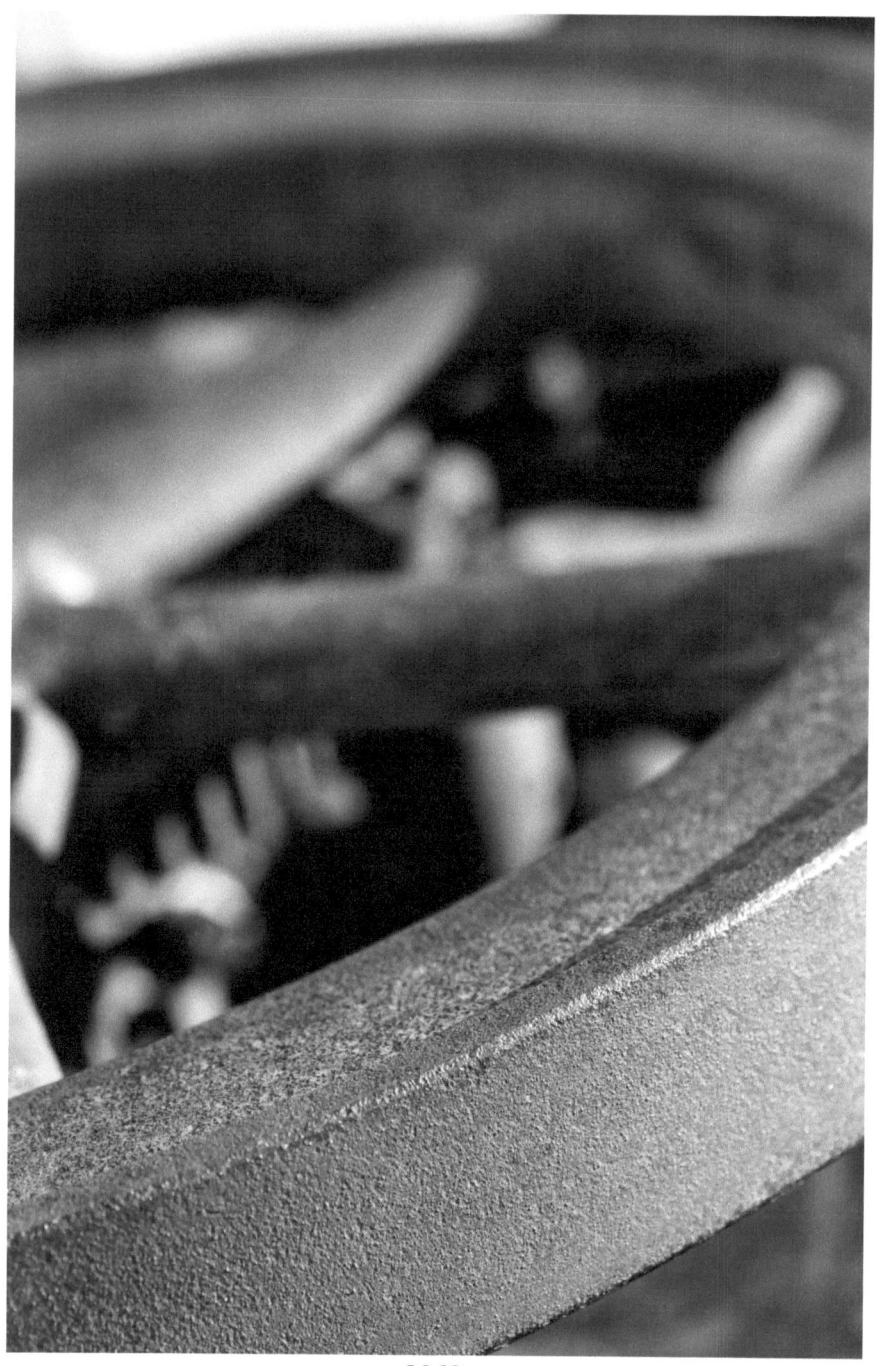

2962

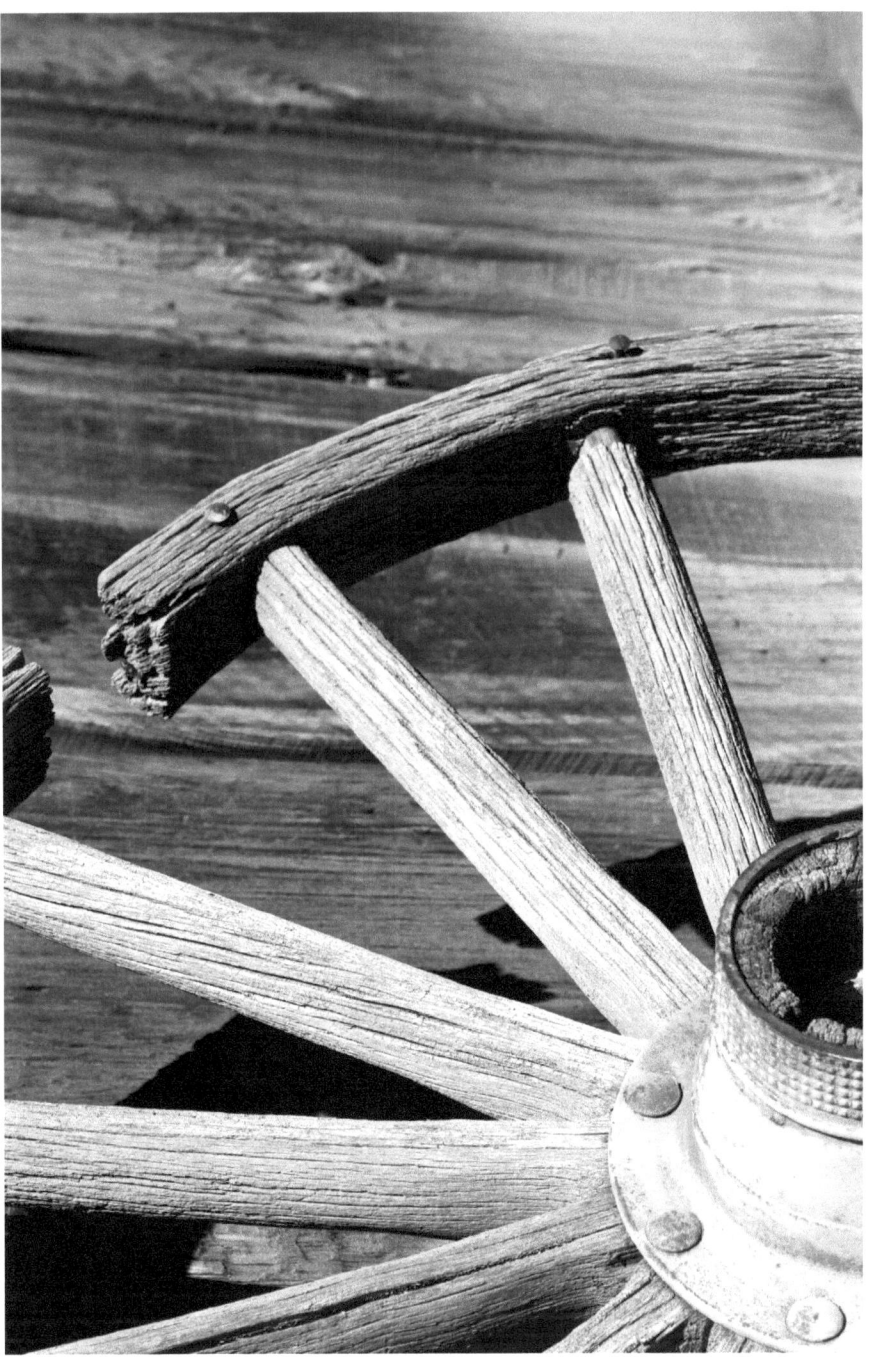

3147

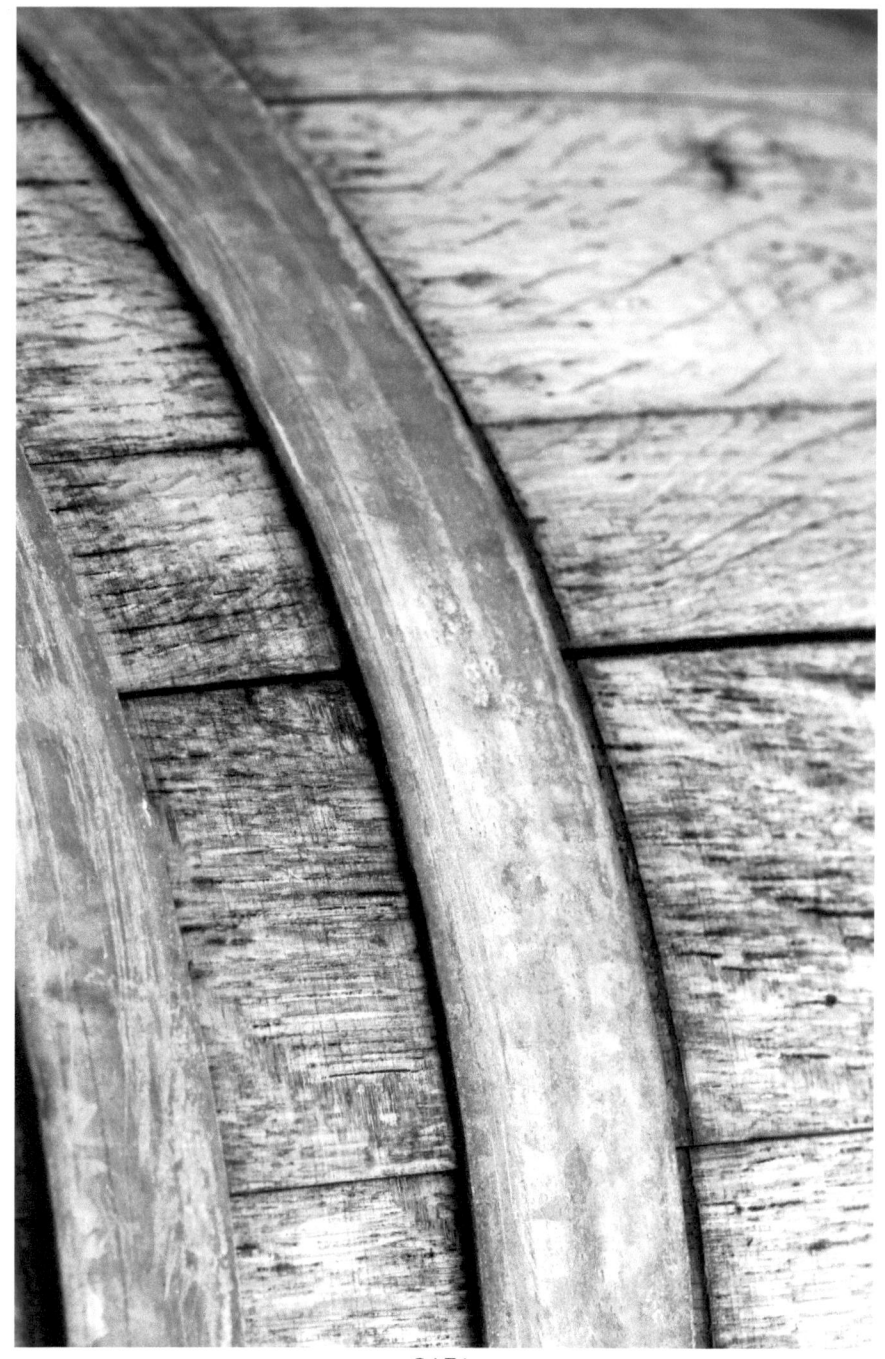

3151

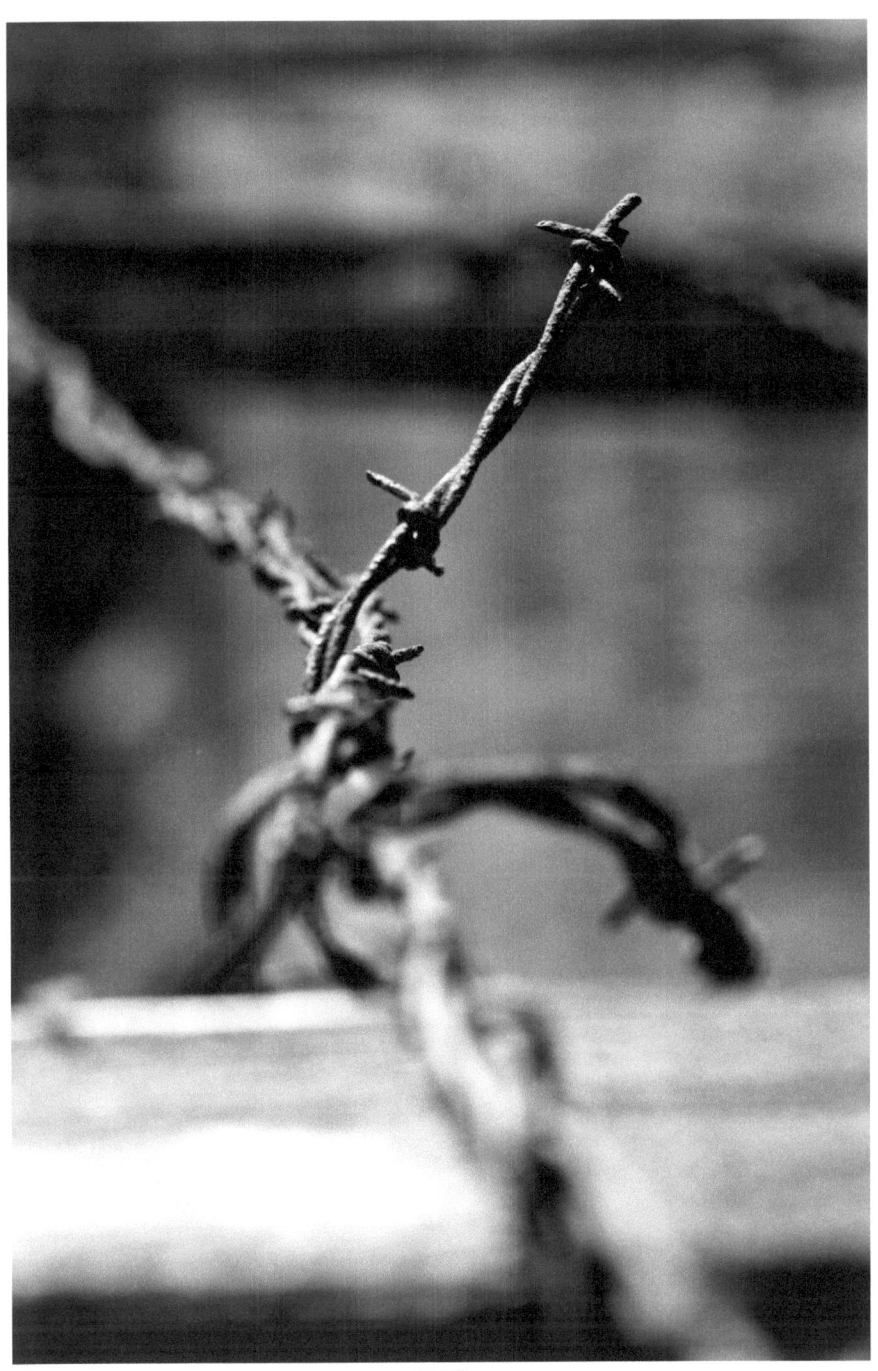

3359

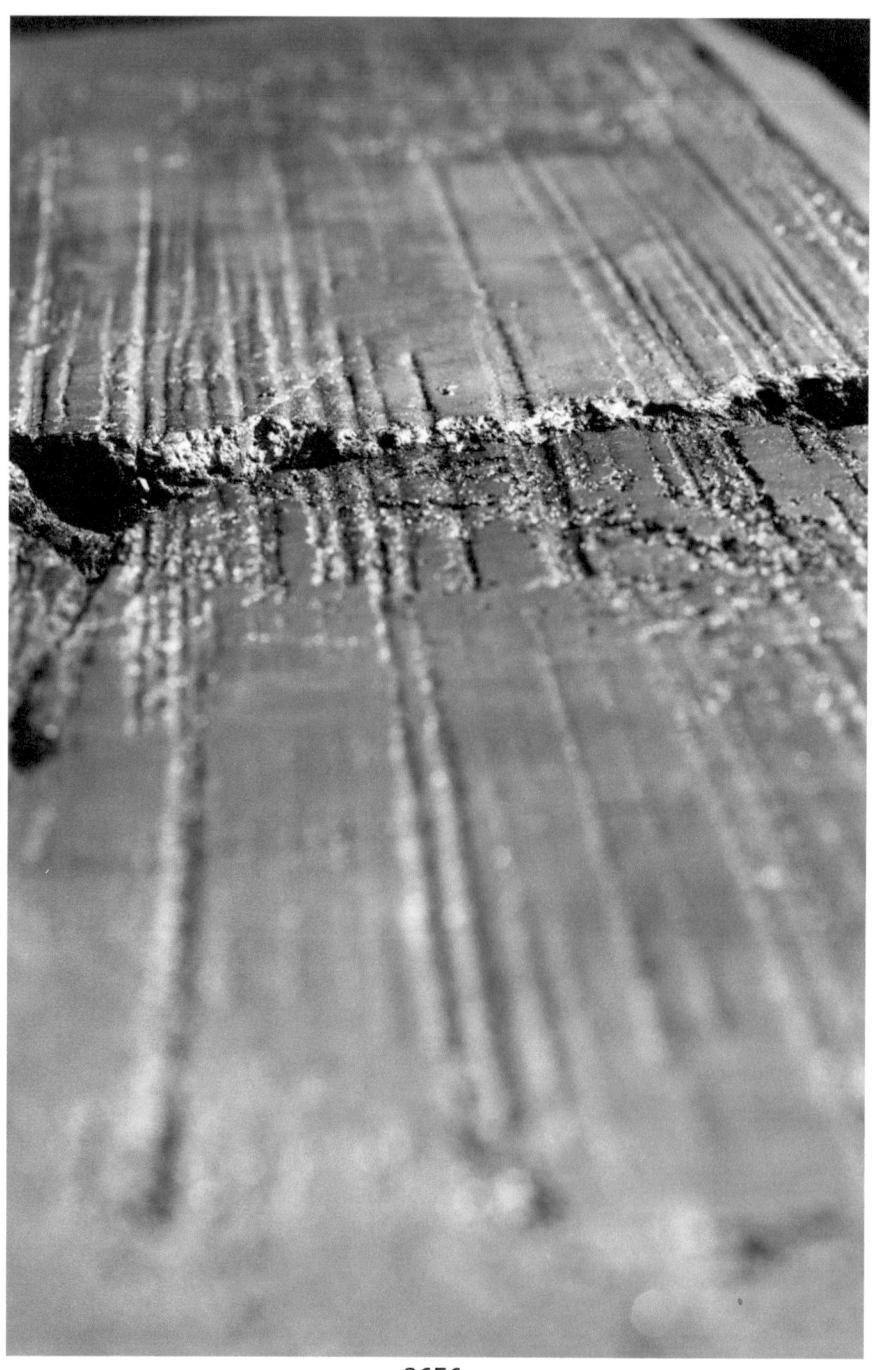

3656

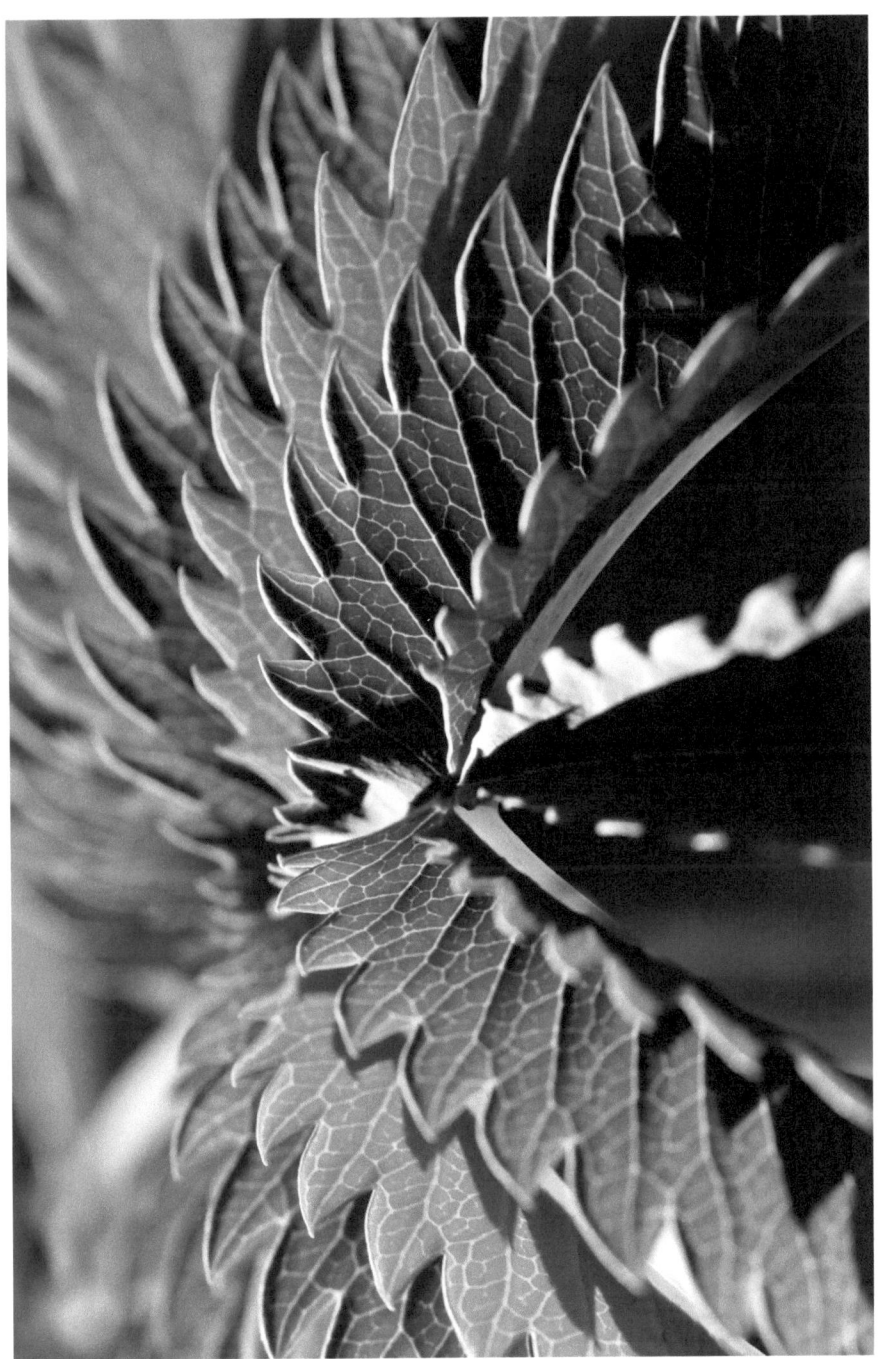

3714

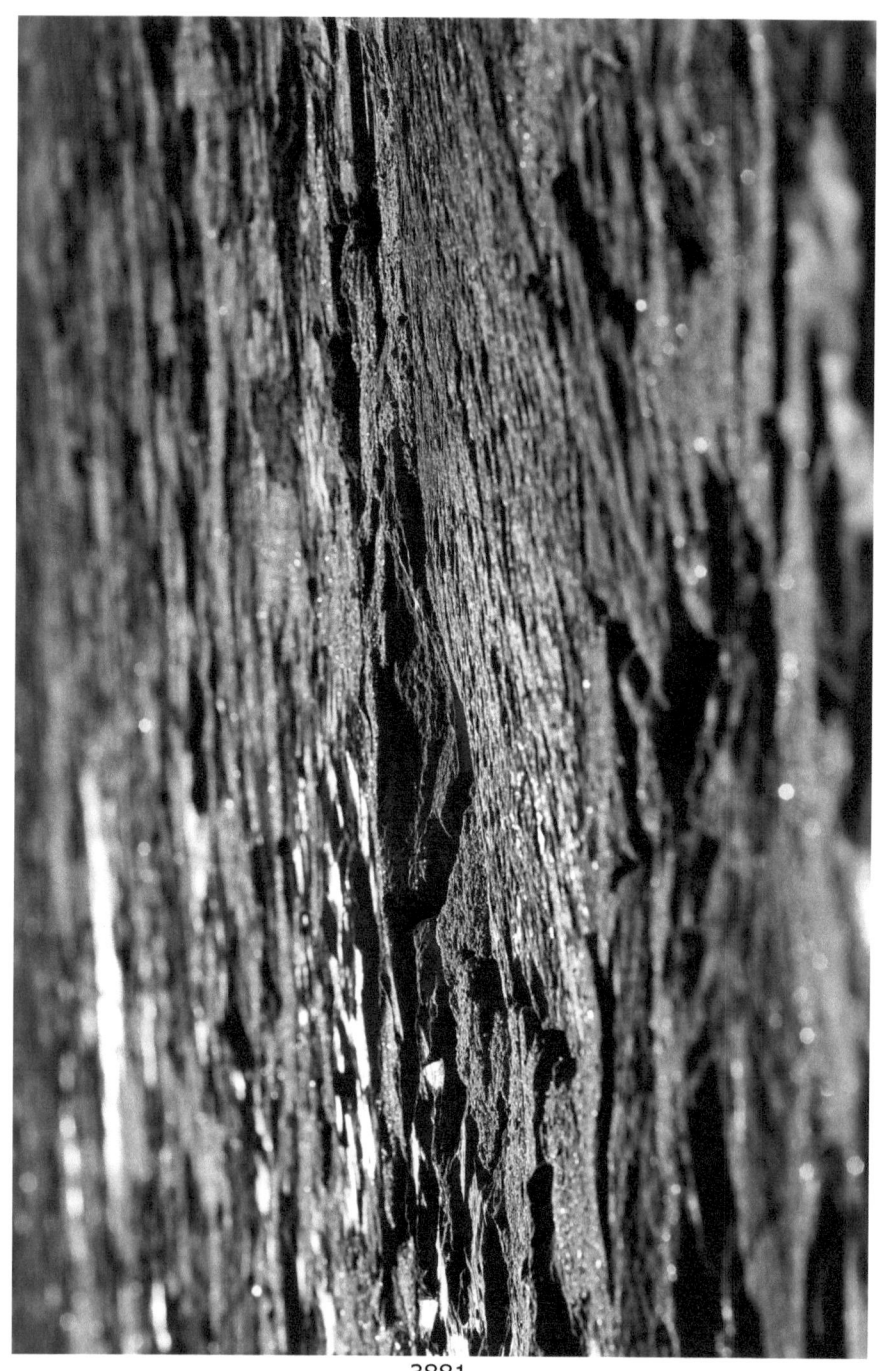

3881

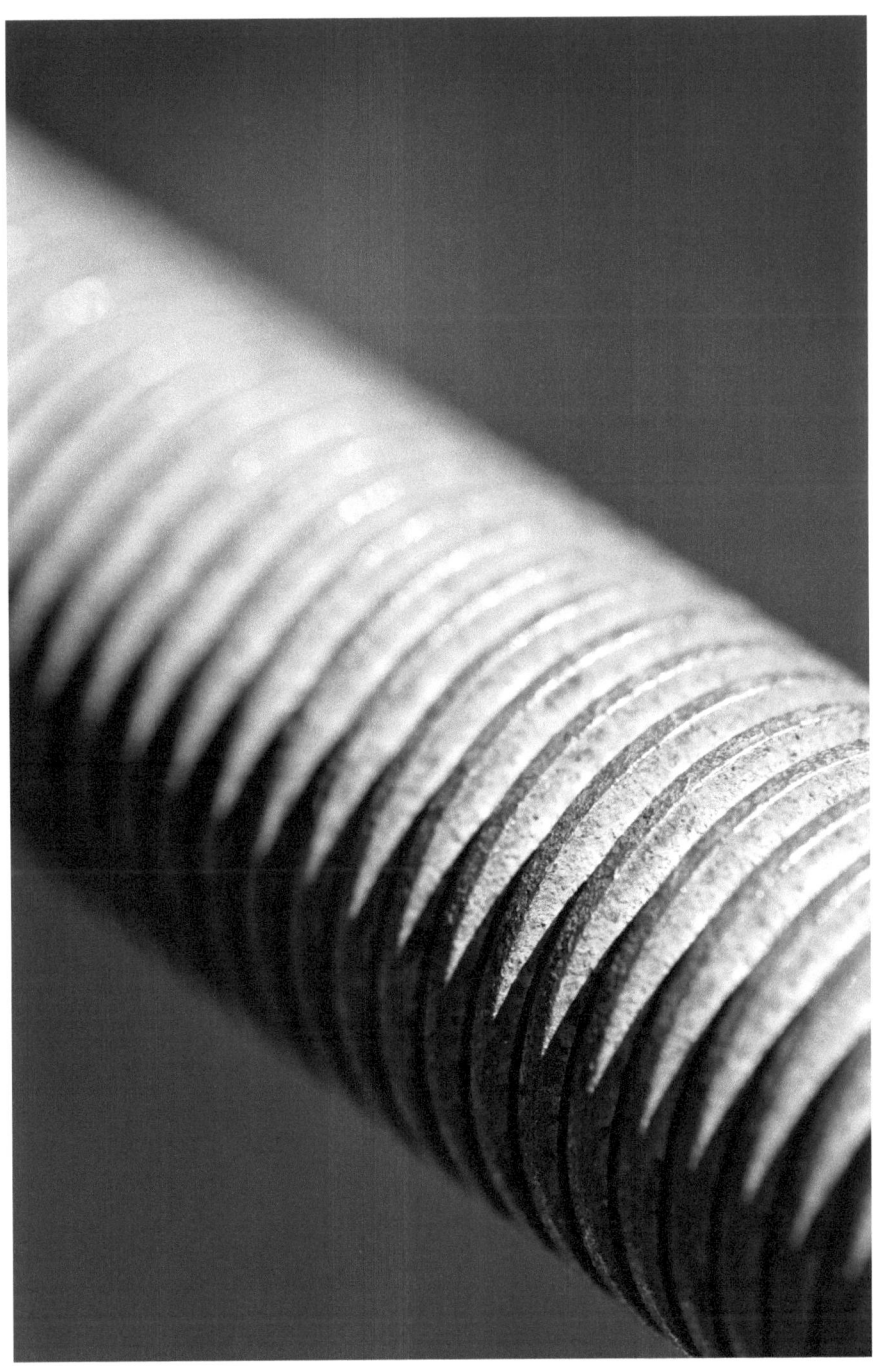

3937

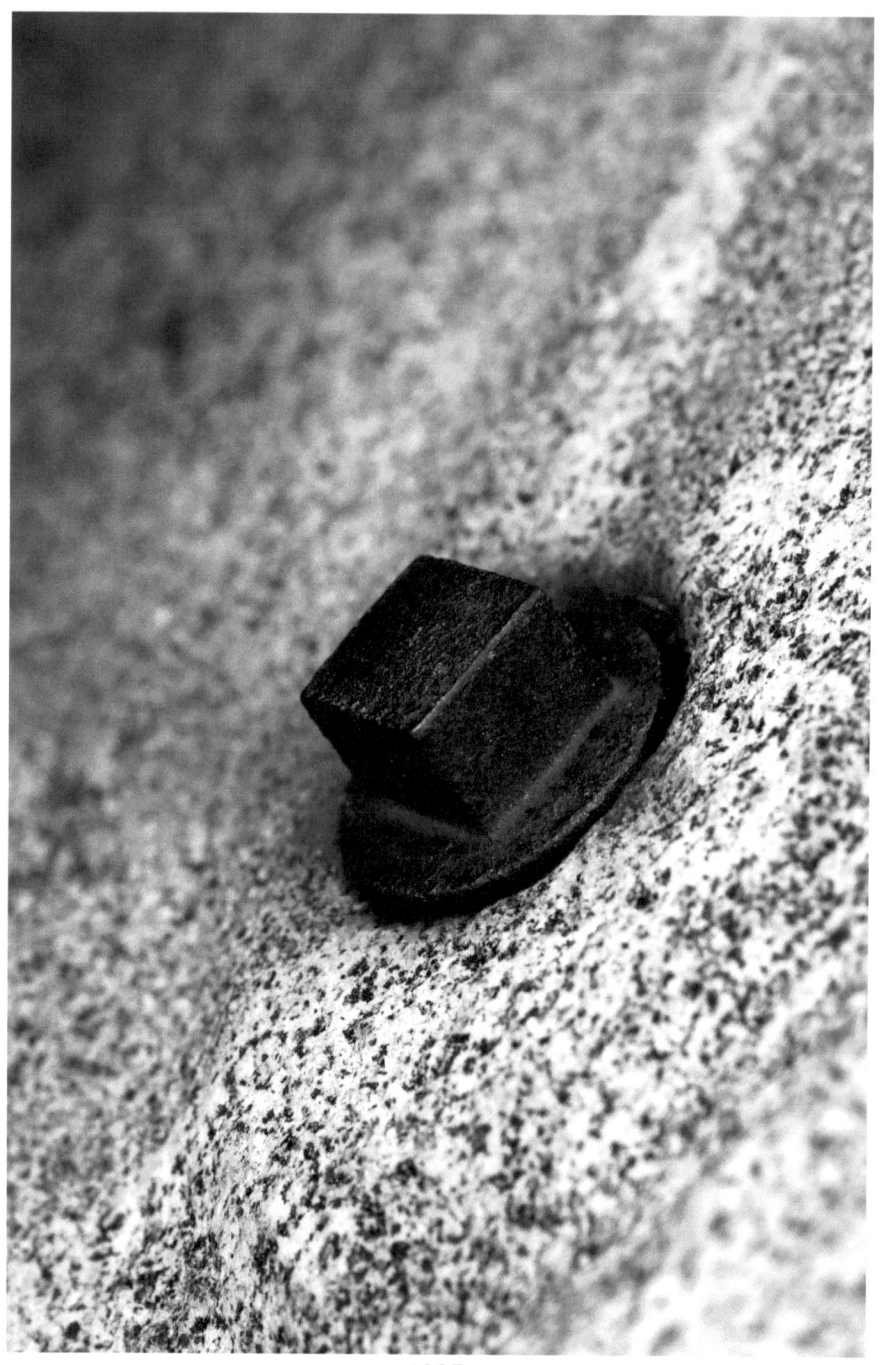

4035

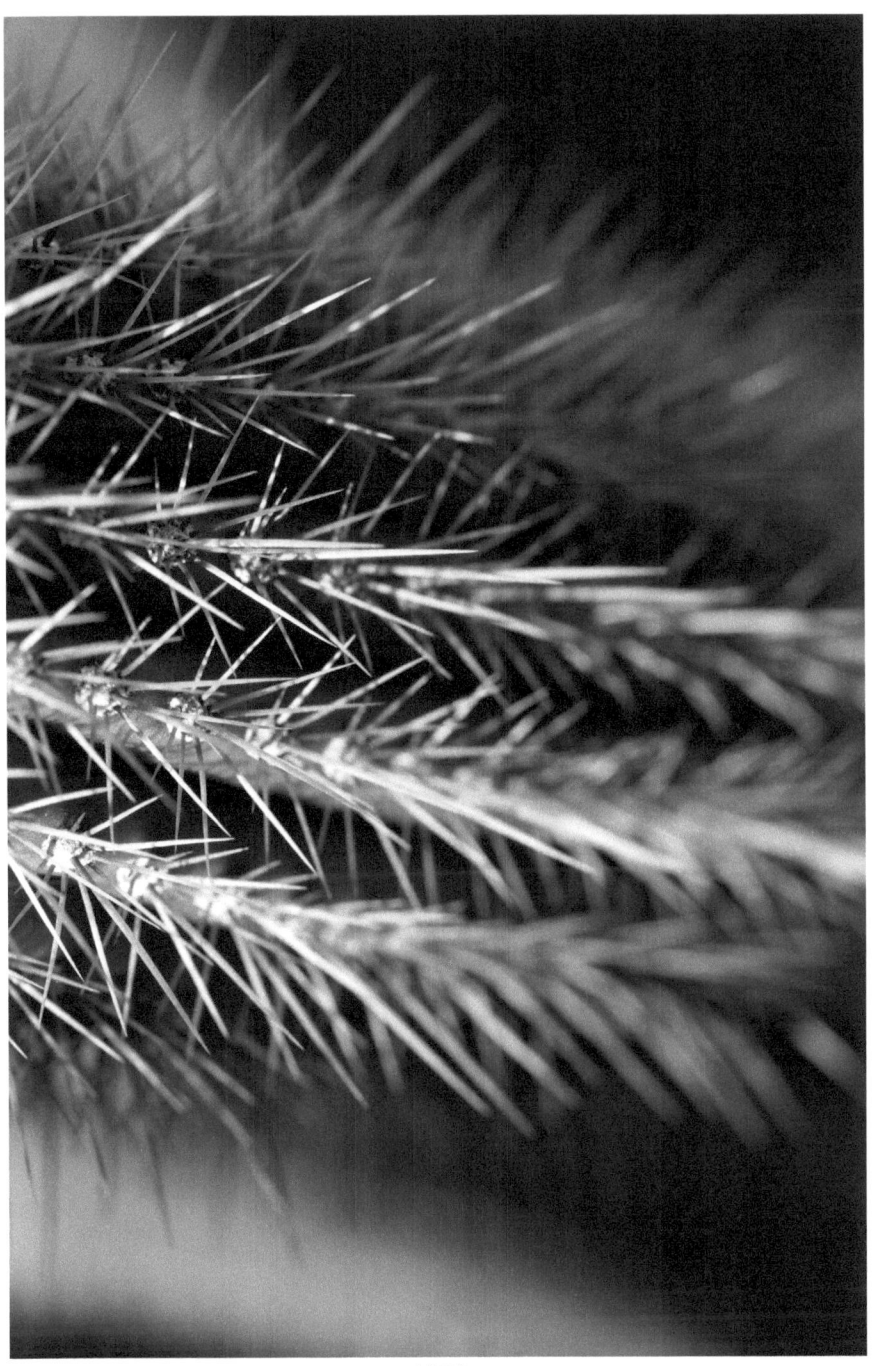

4070

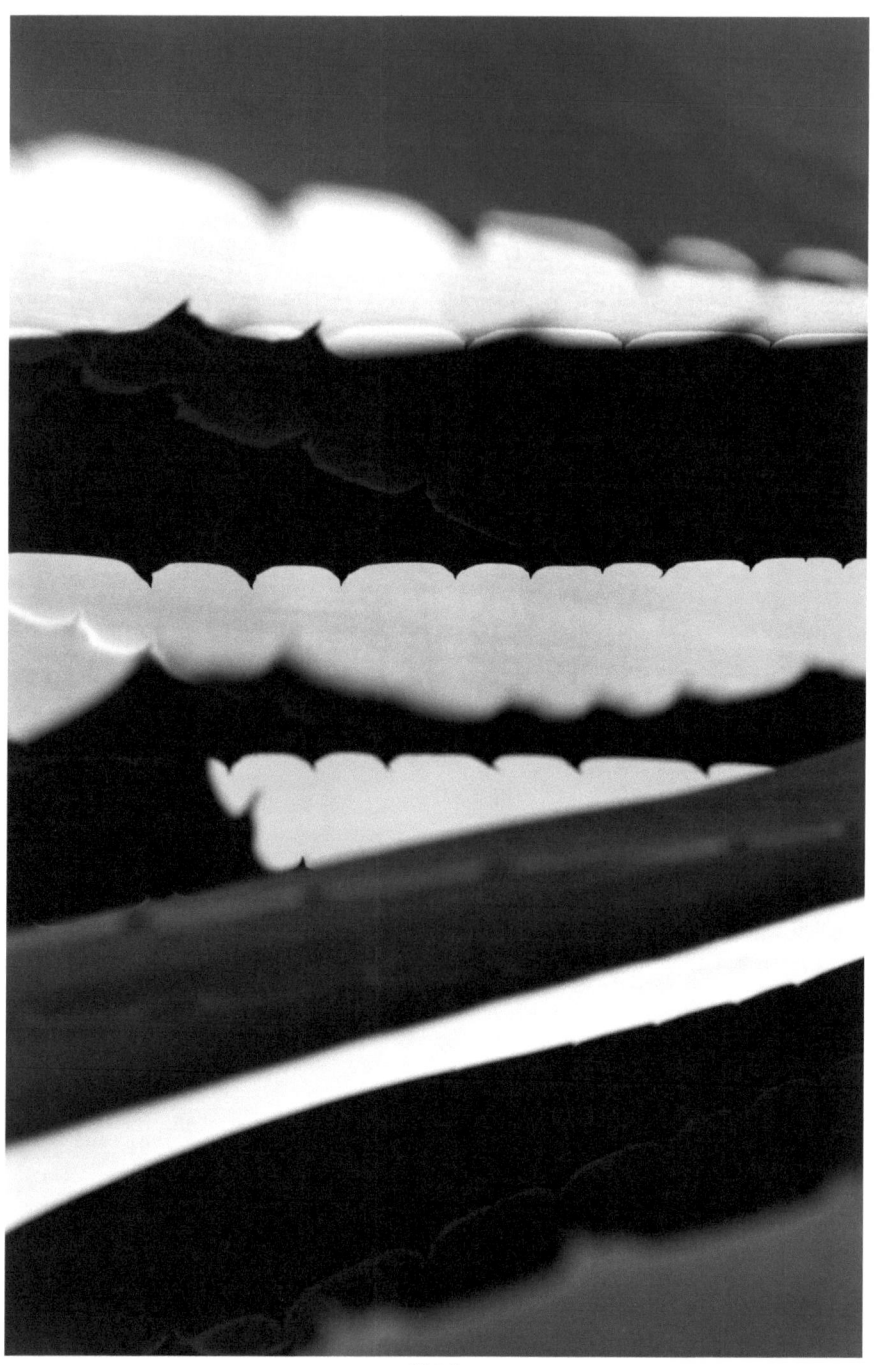

4099

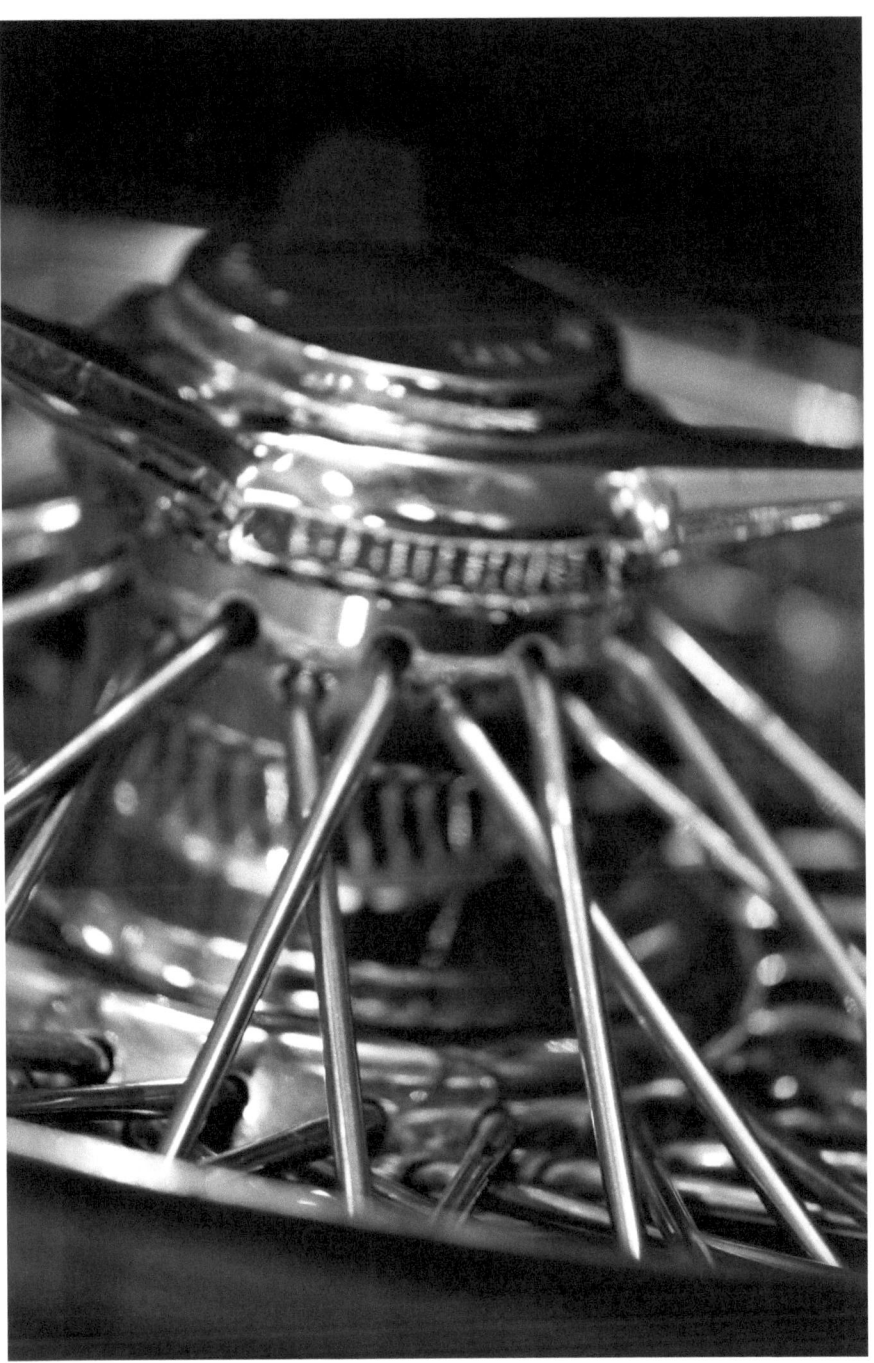

4193

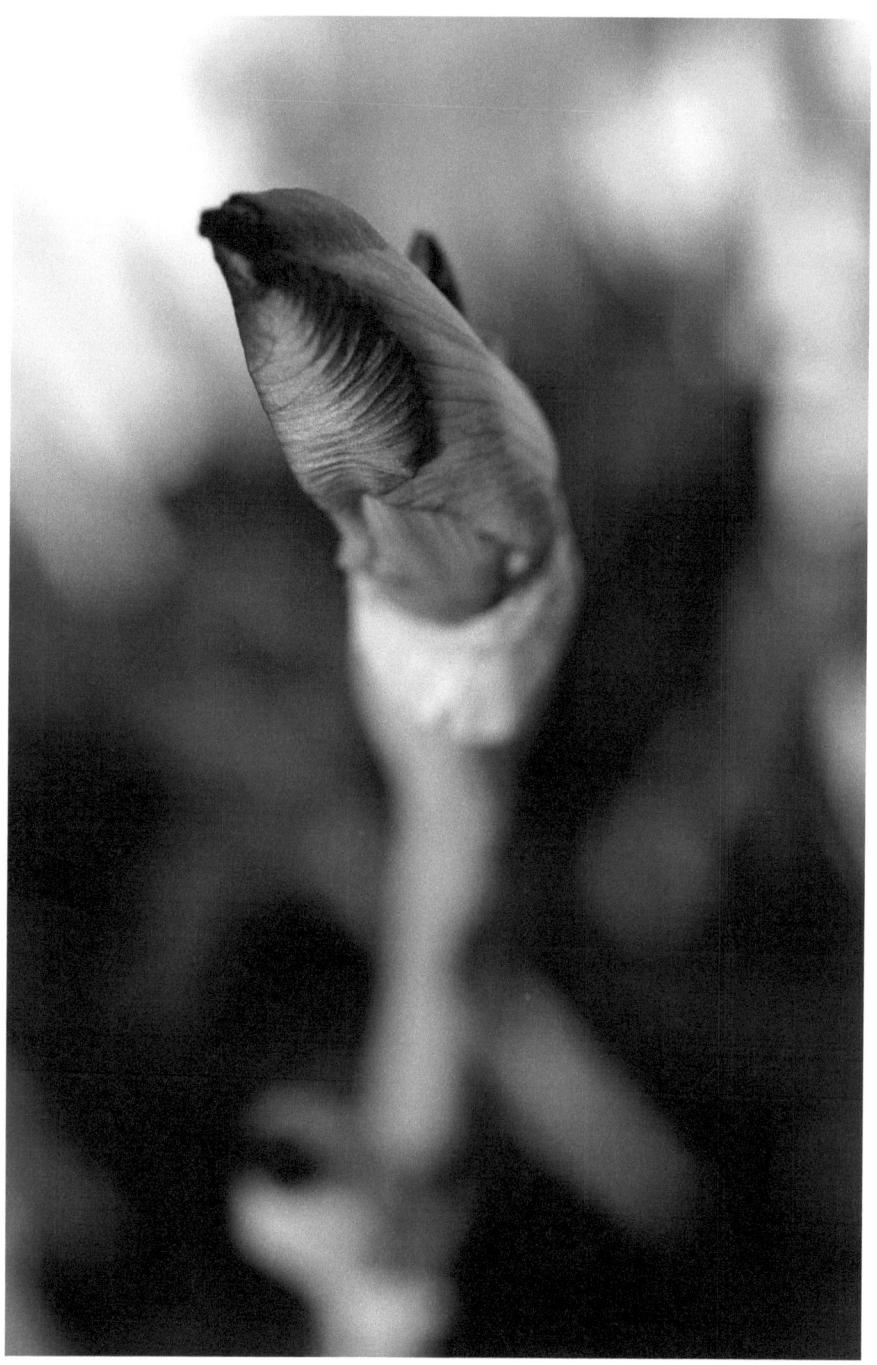

5492

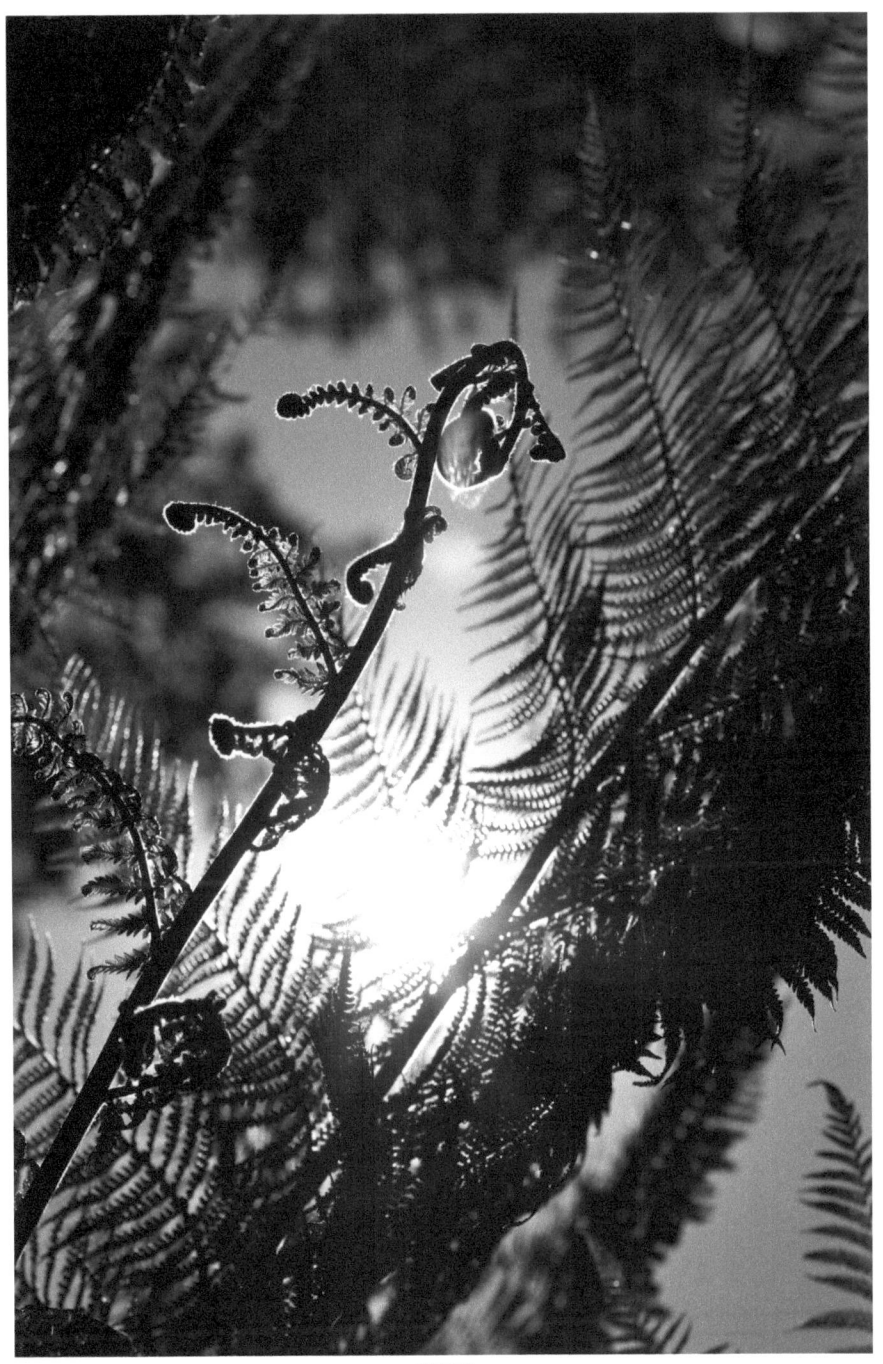

5705

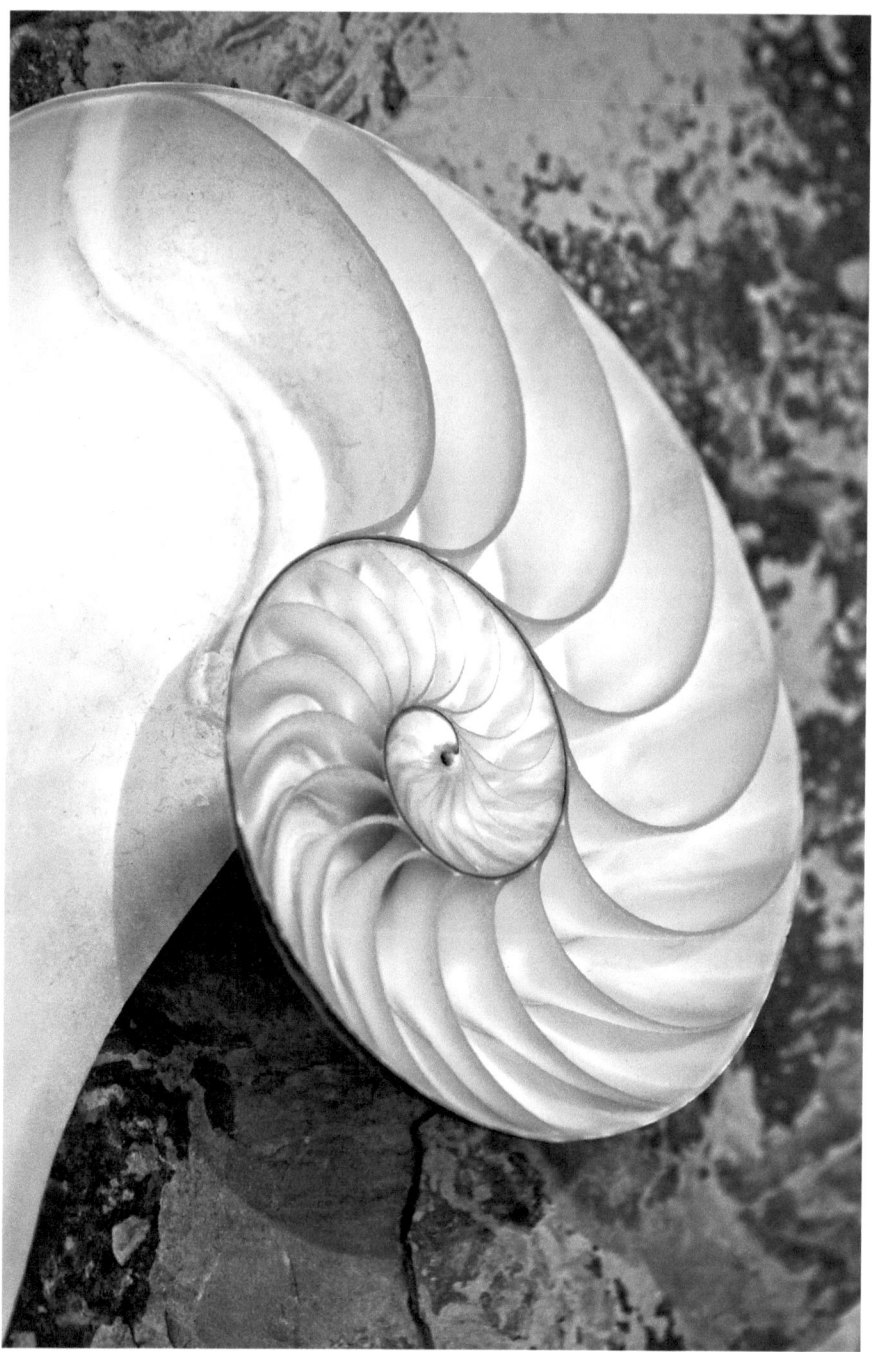

5708

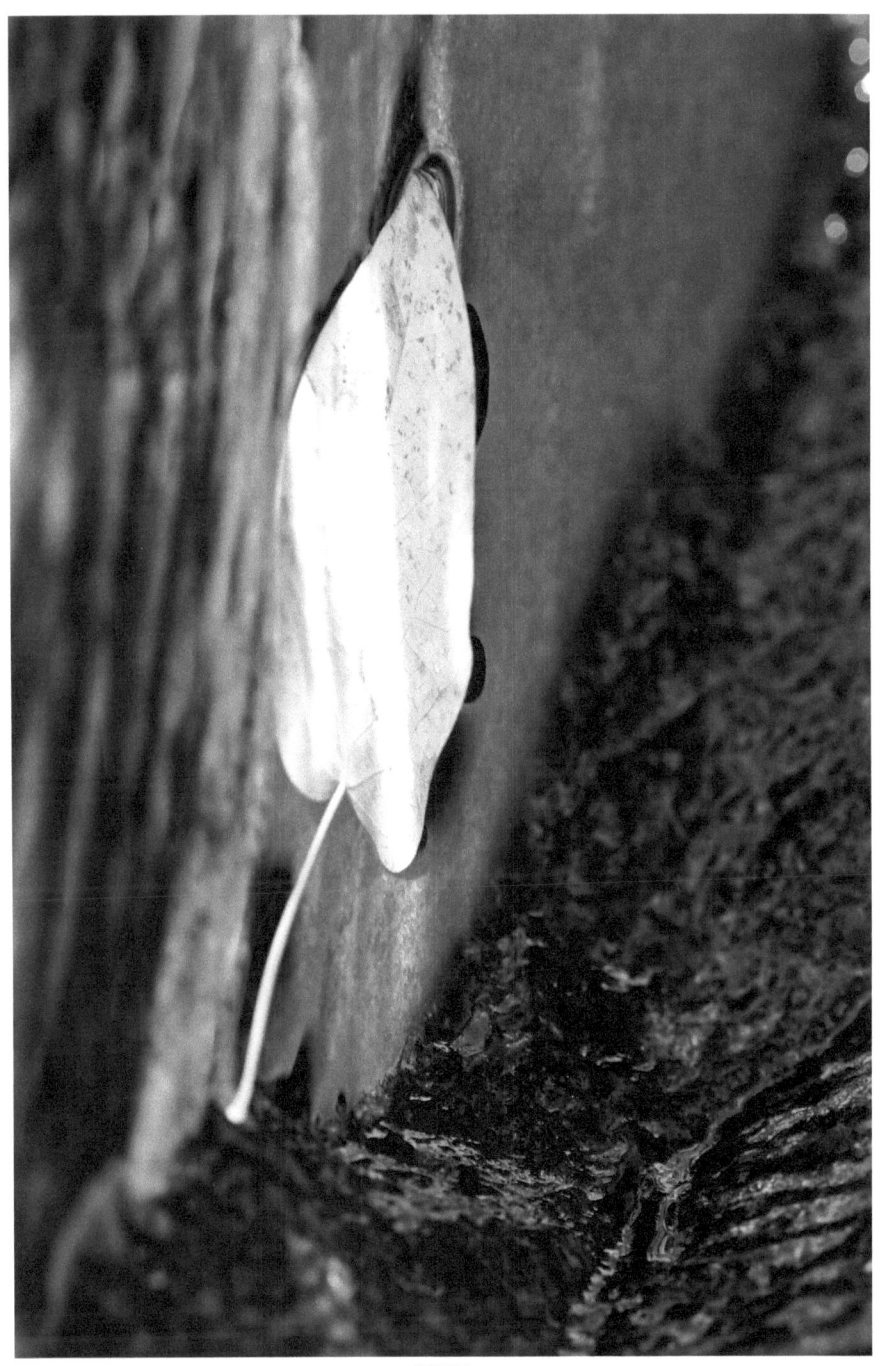

5750

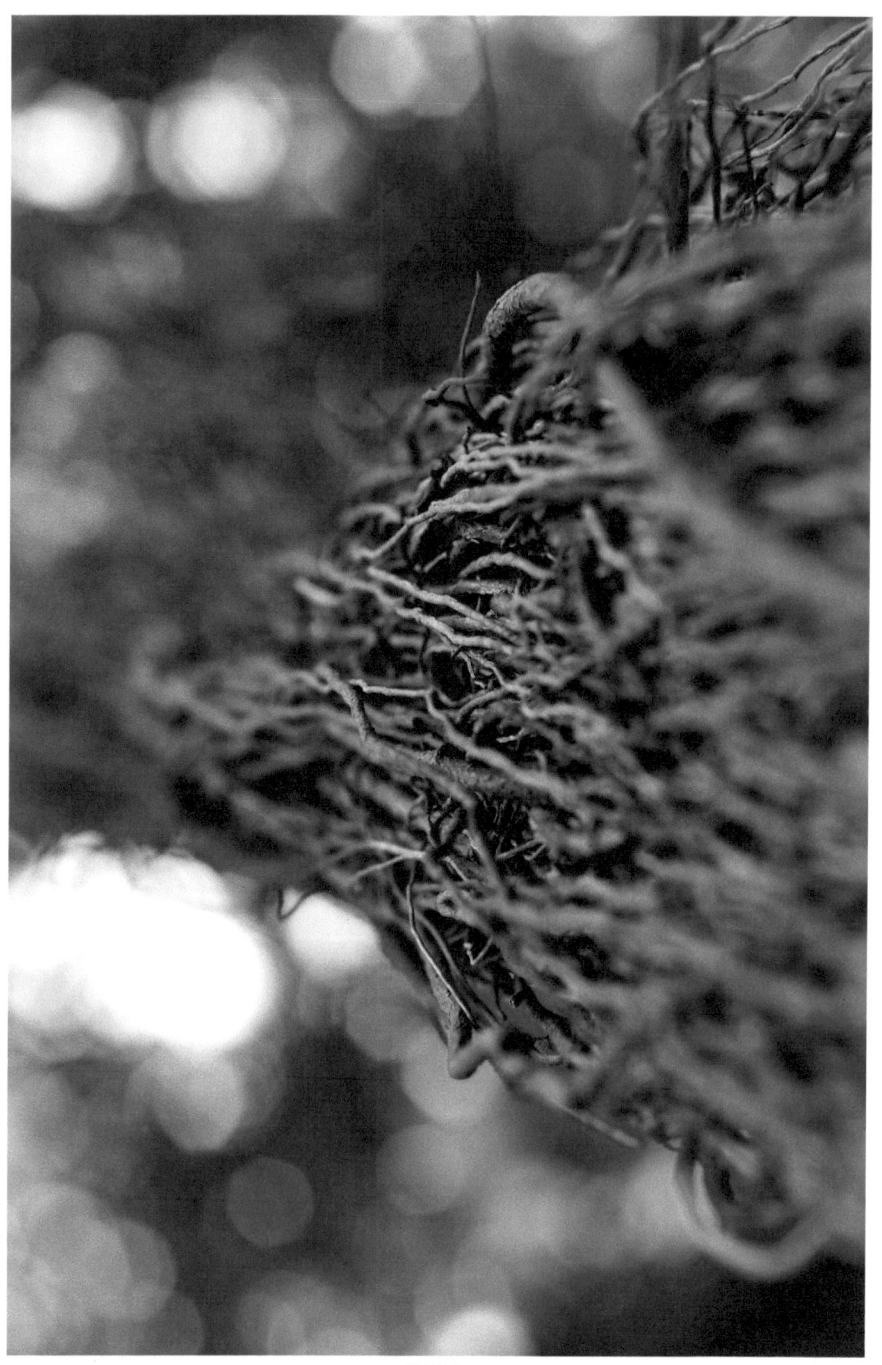

5811

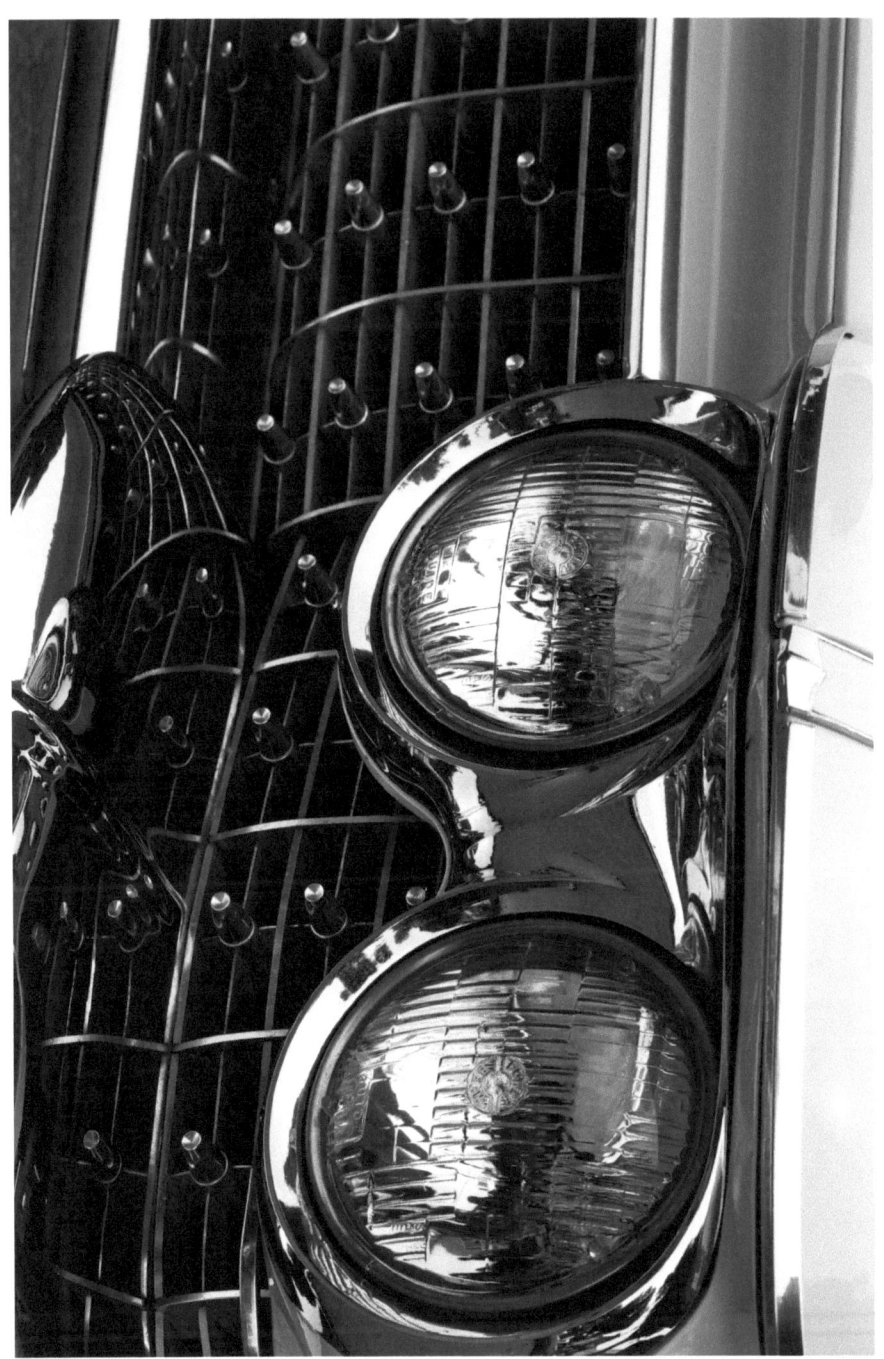

5844

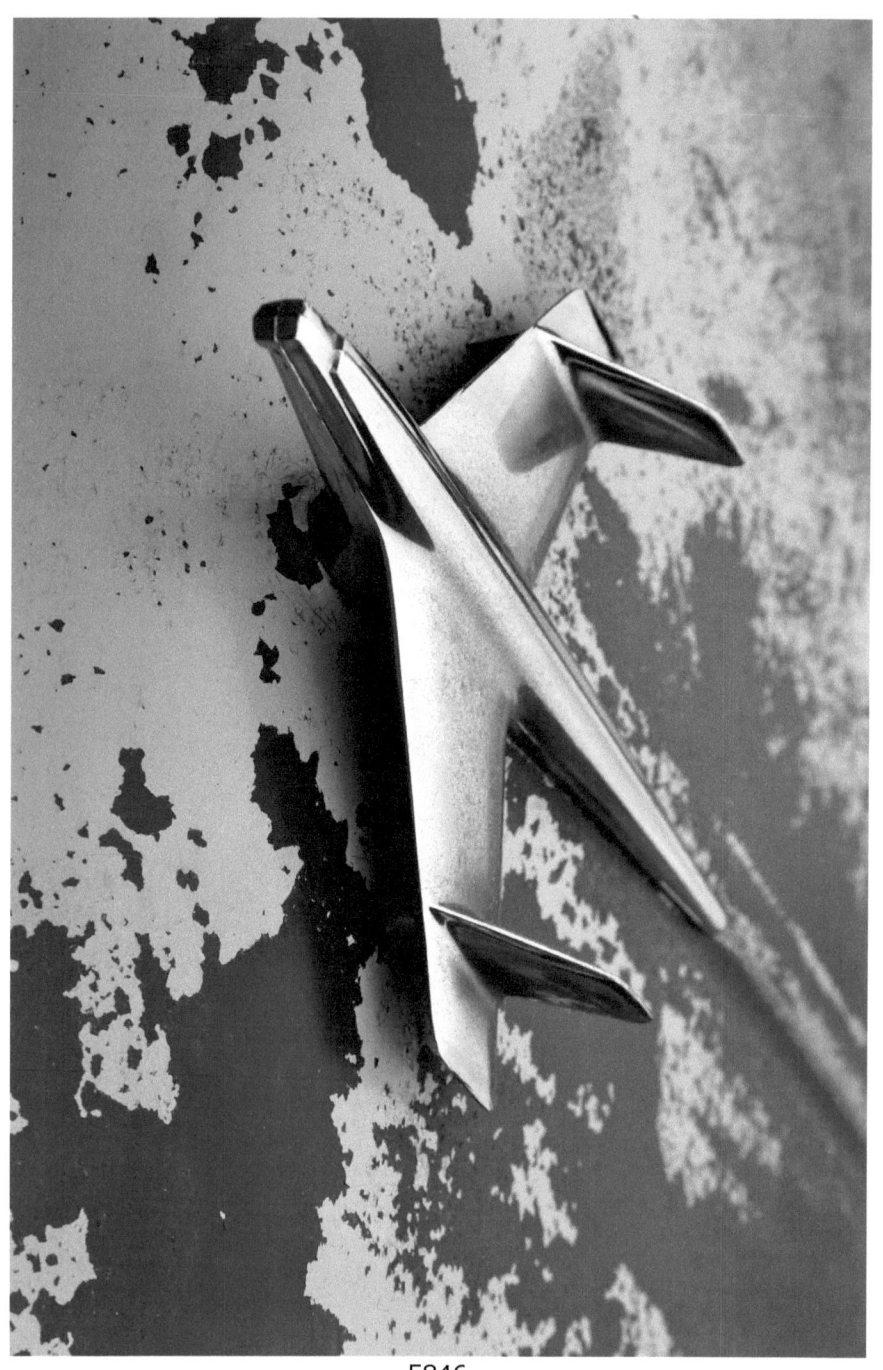

5846

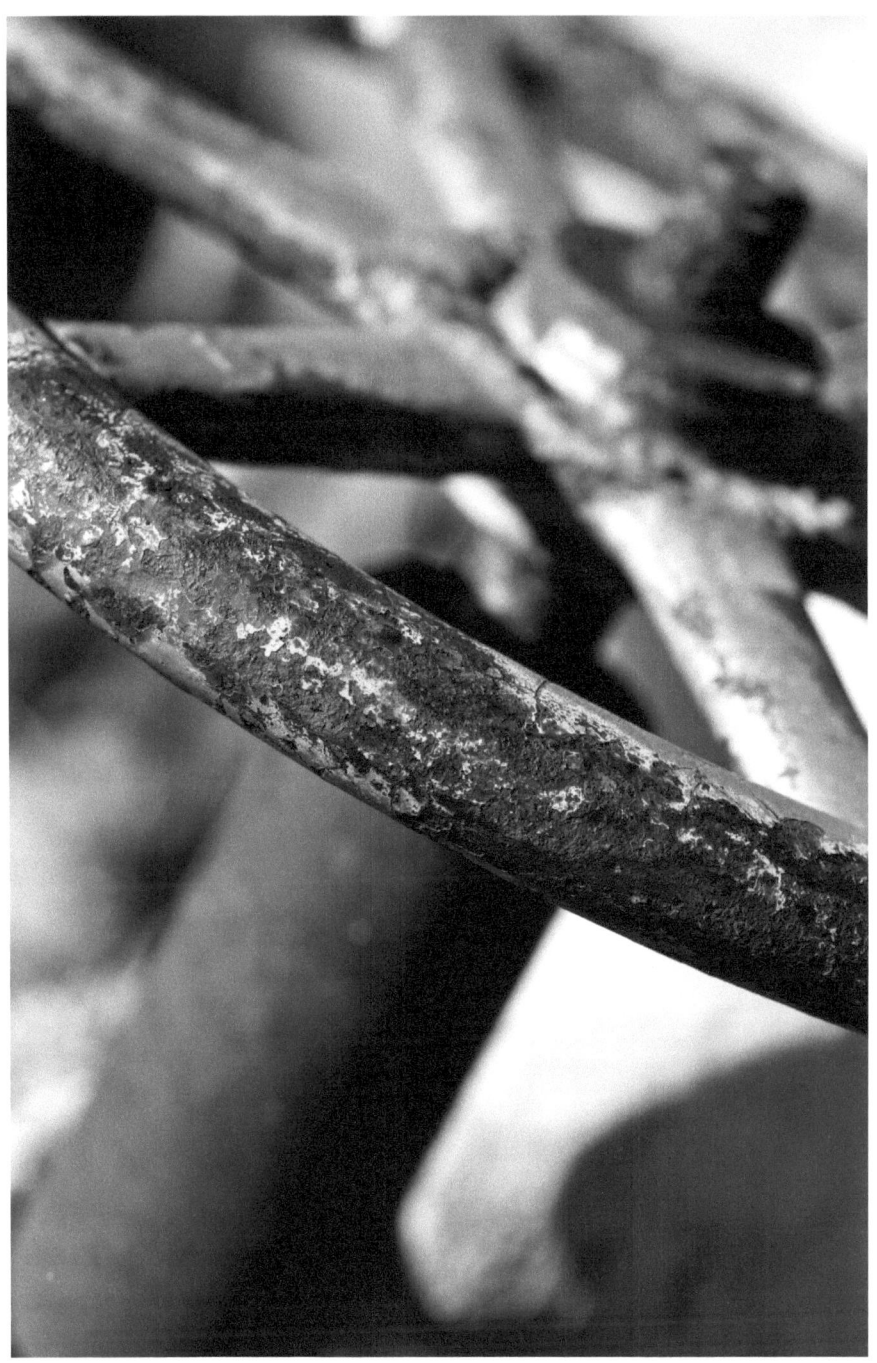

6095

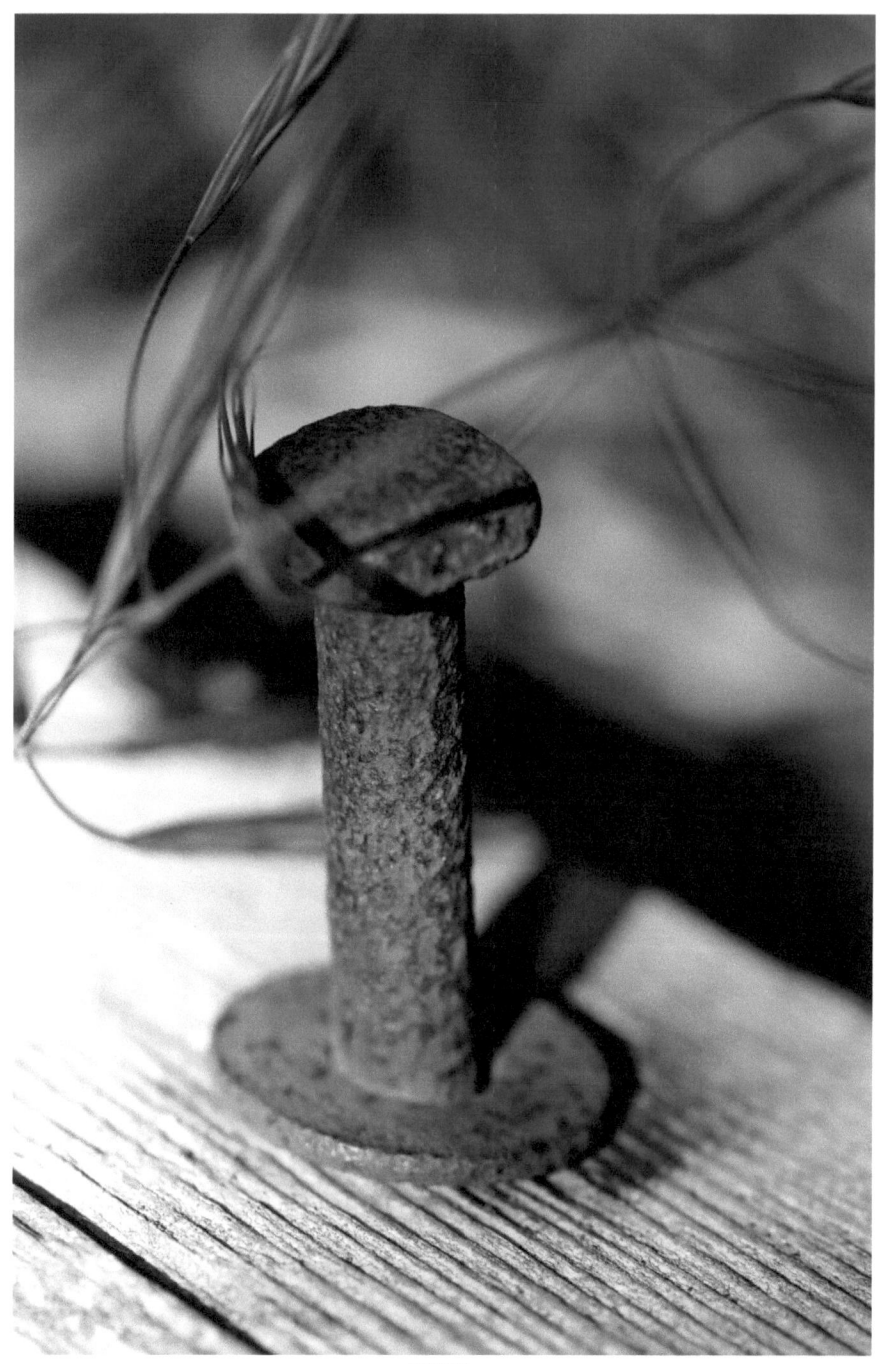

7182

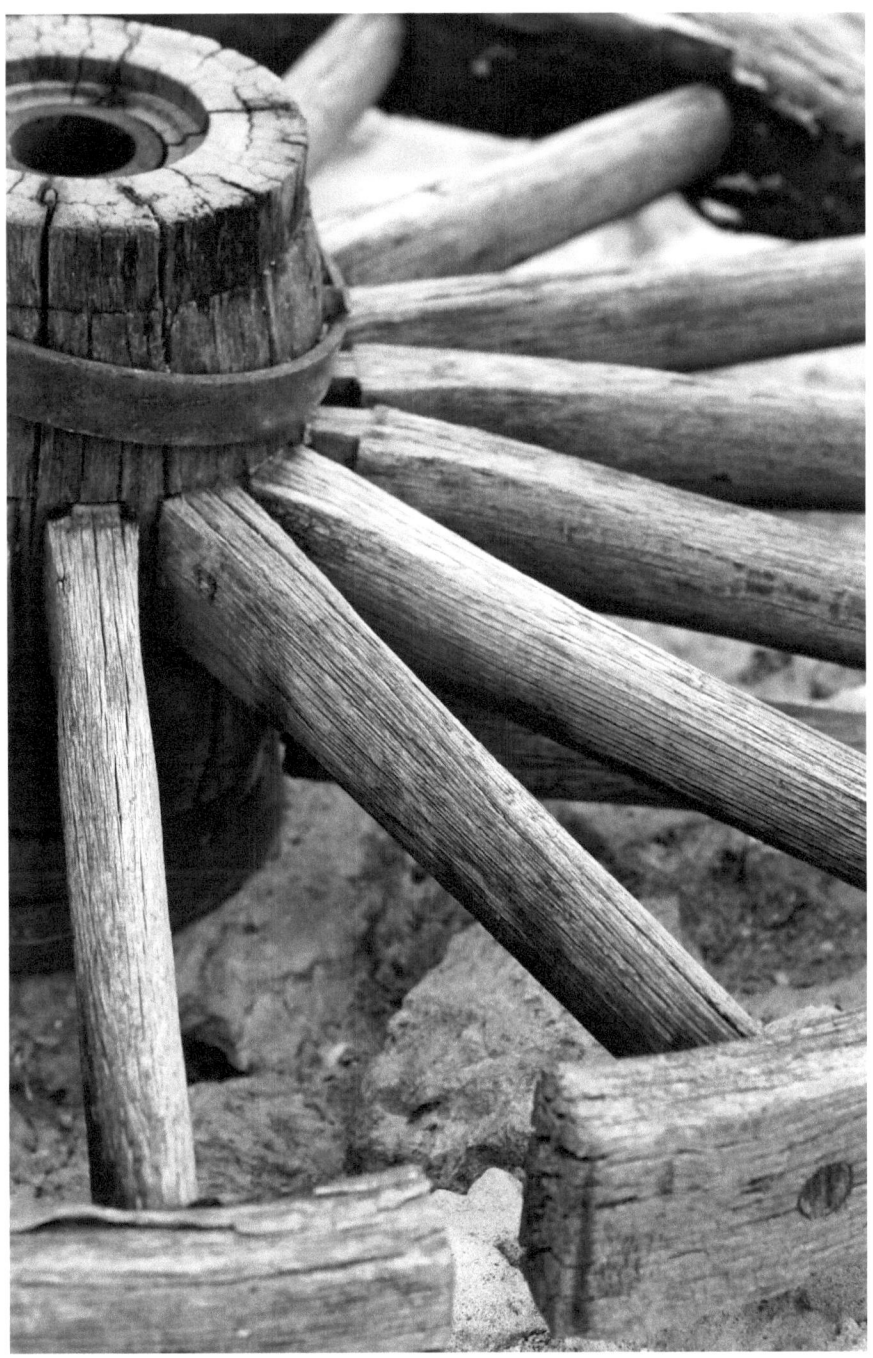

7783

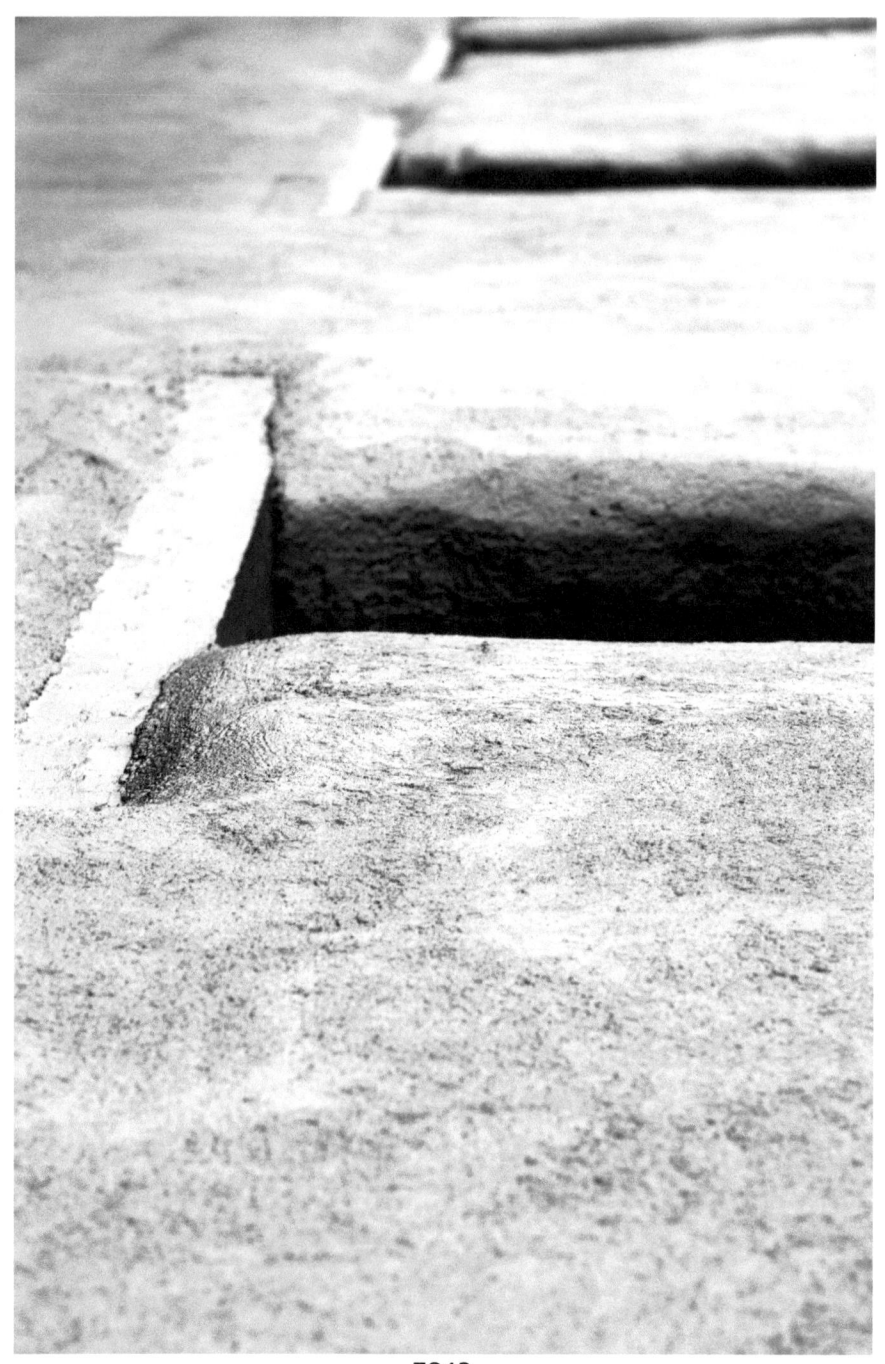

7843

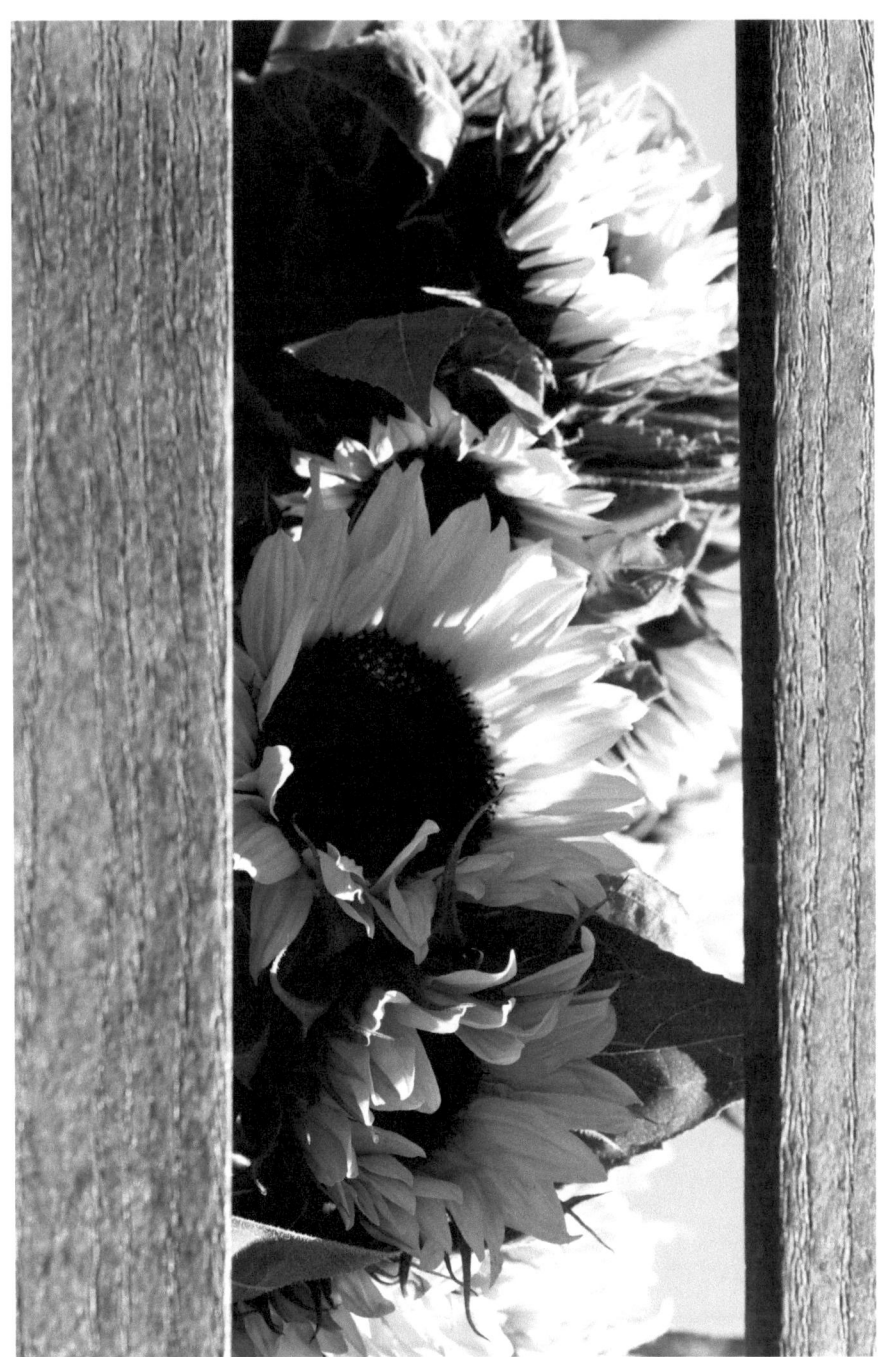

8345

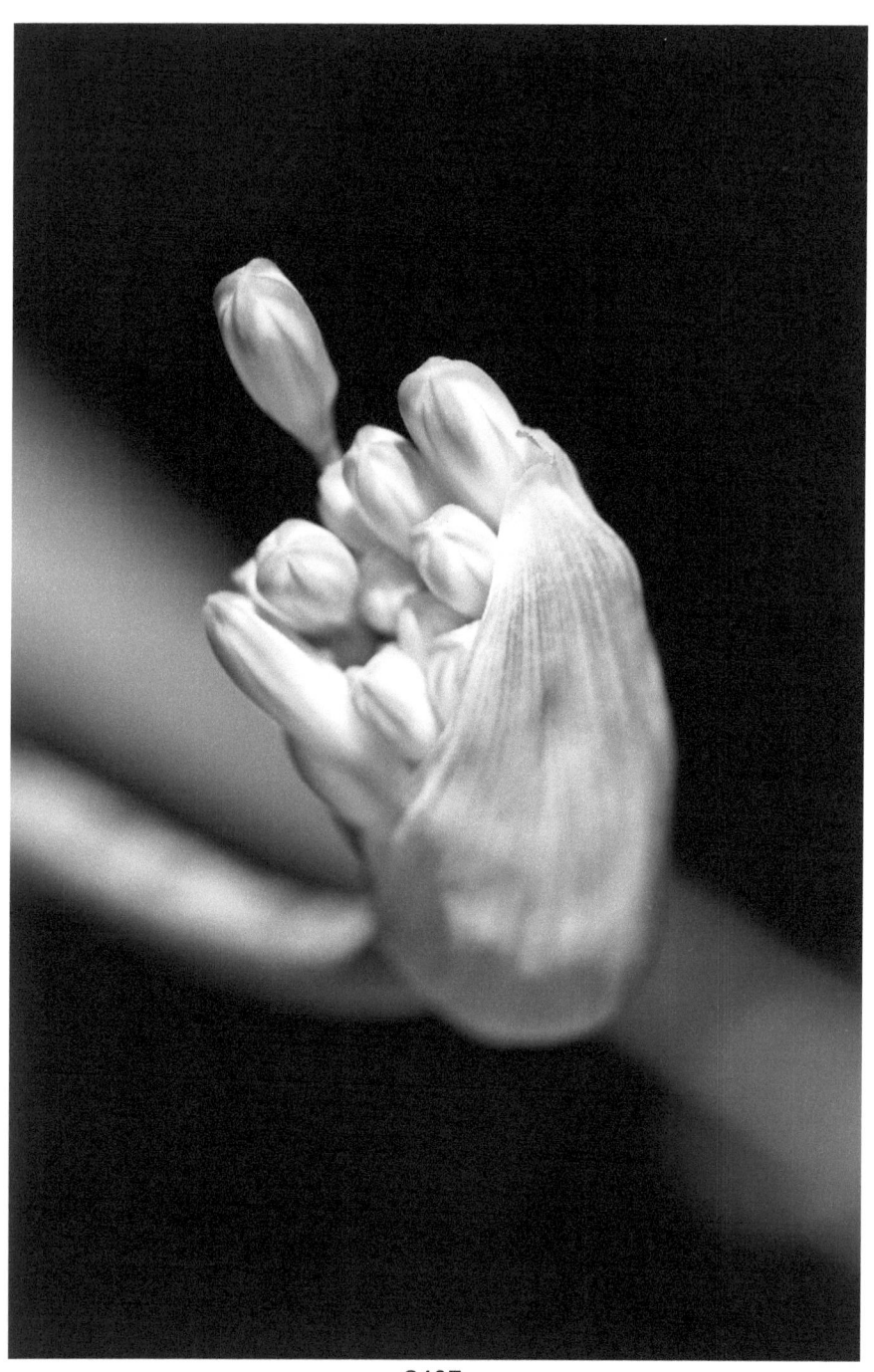

8407

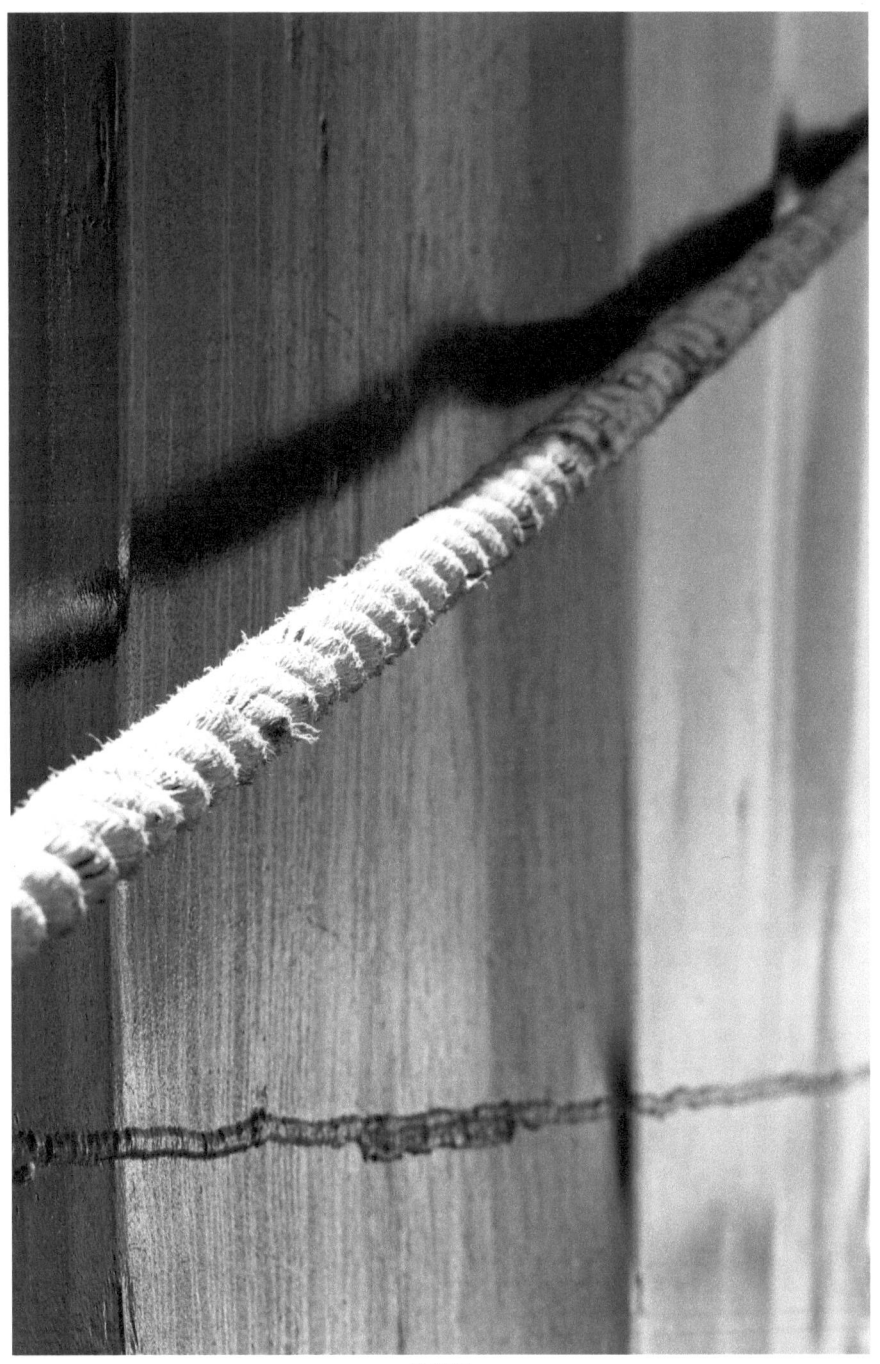

8470

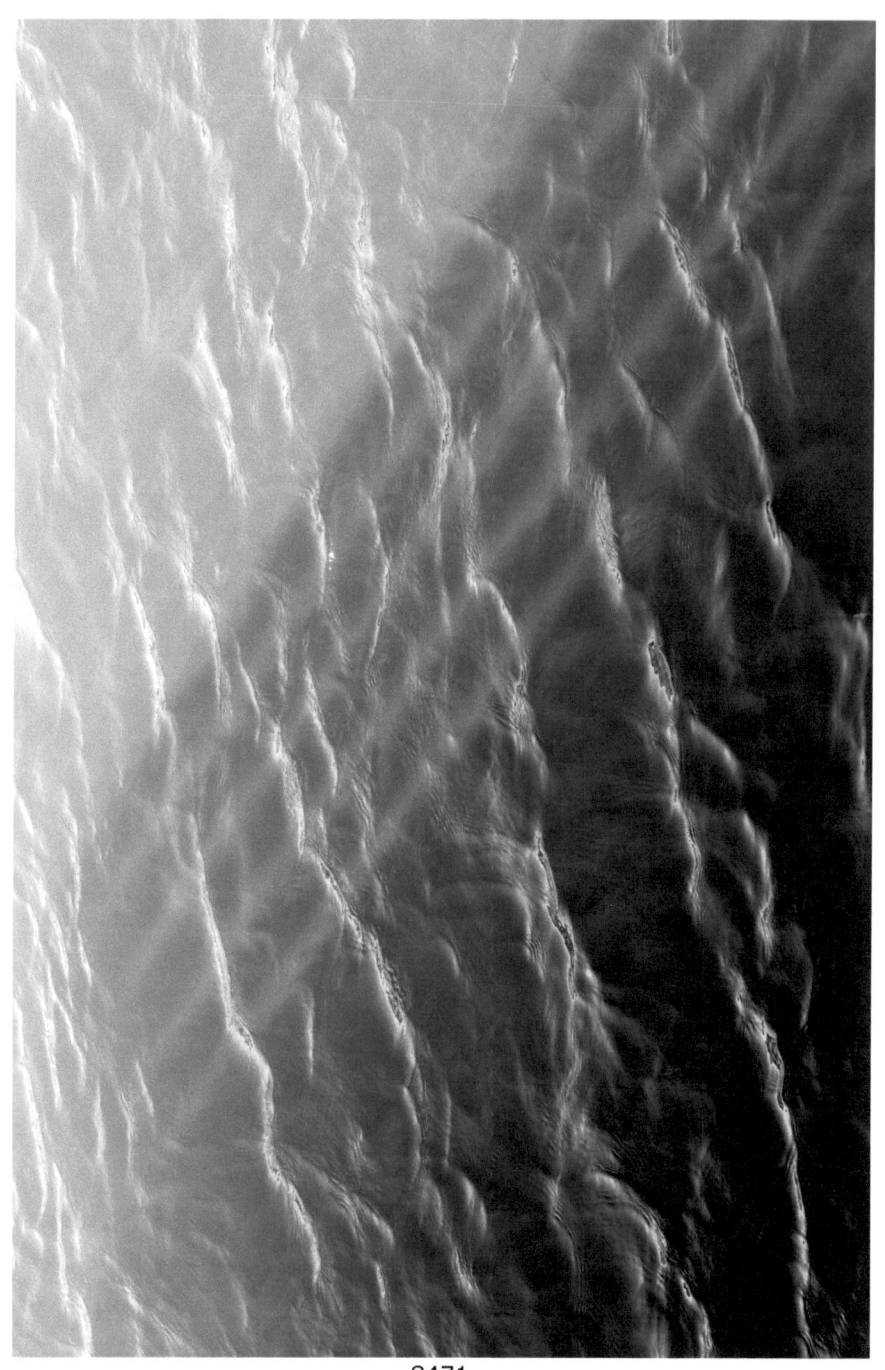

8471

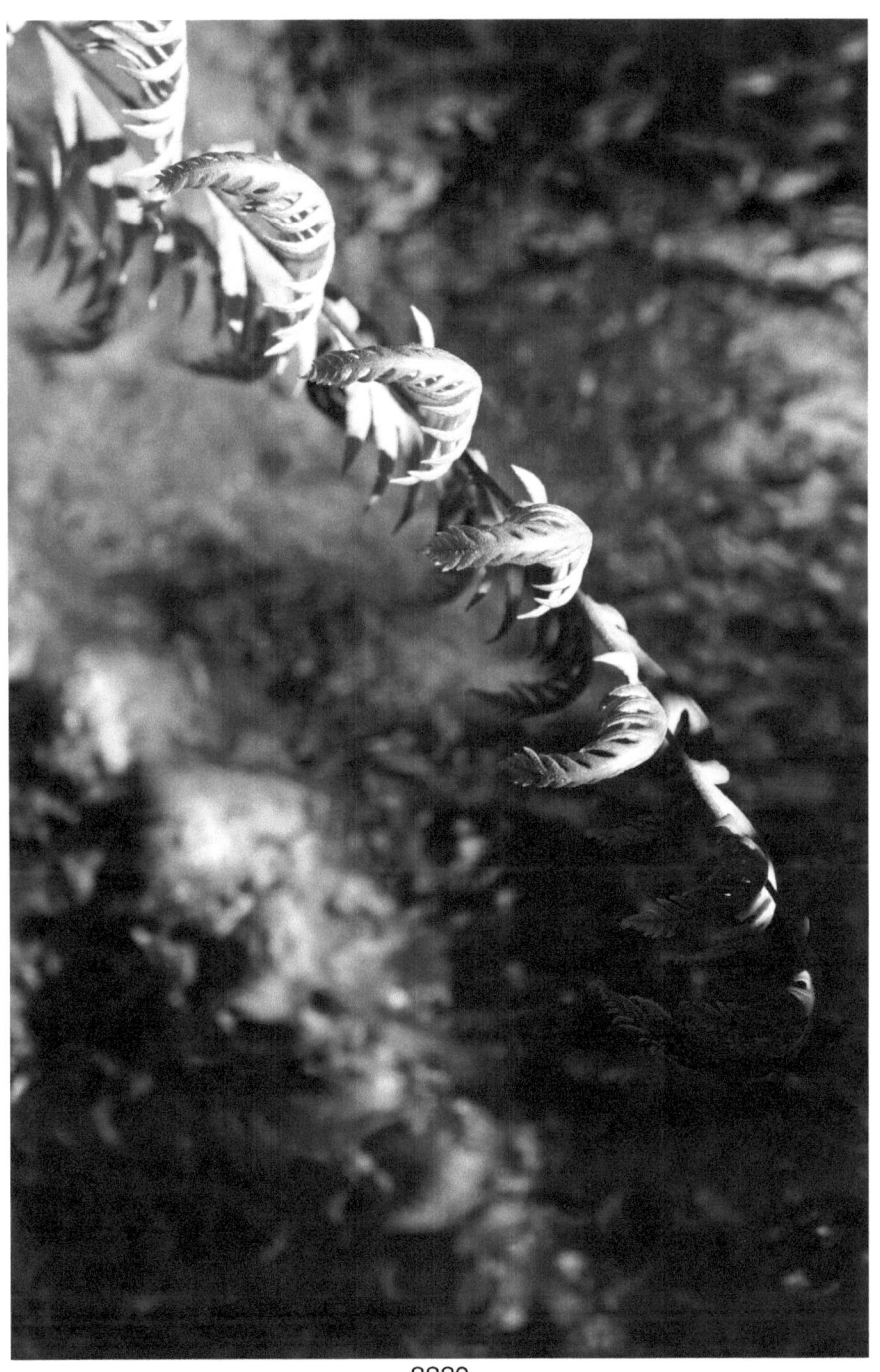

8889

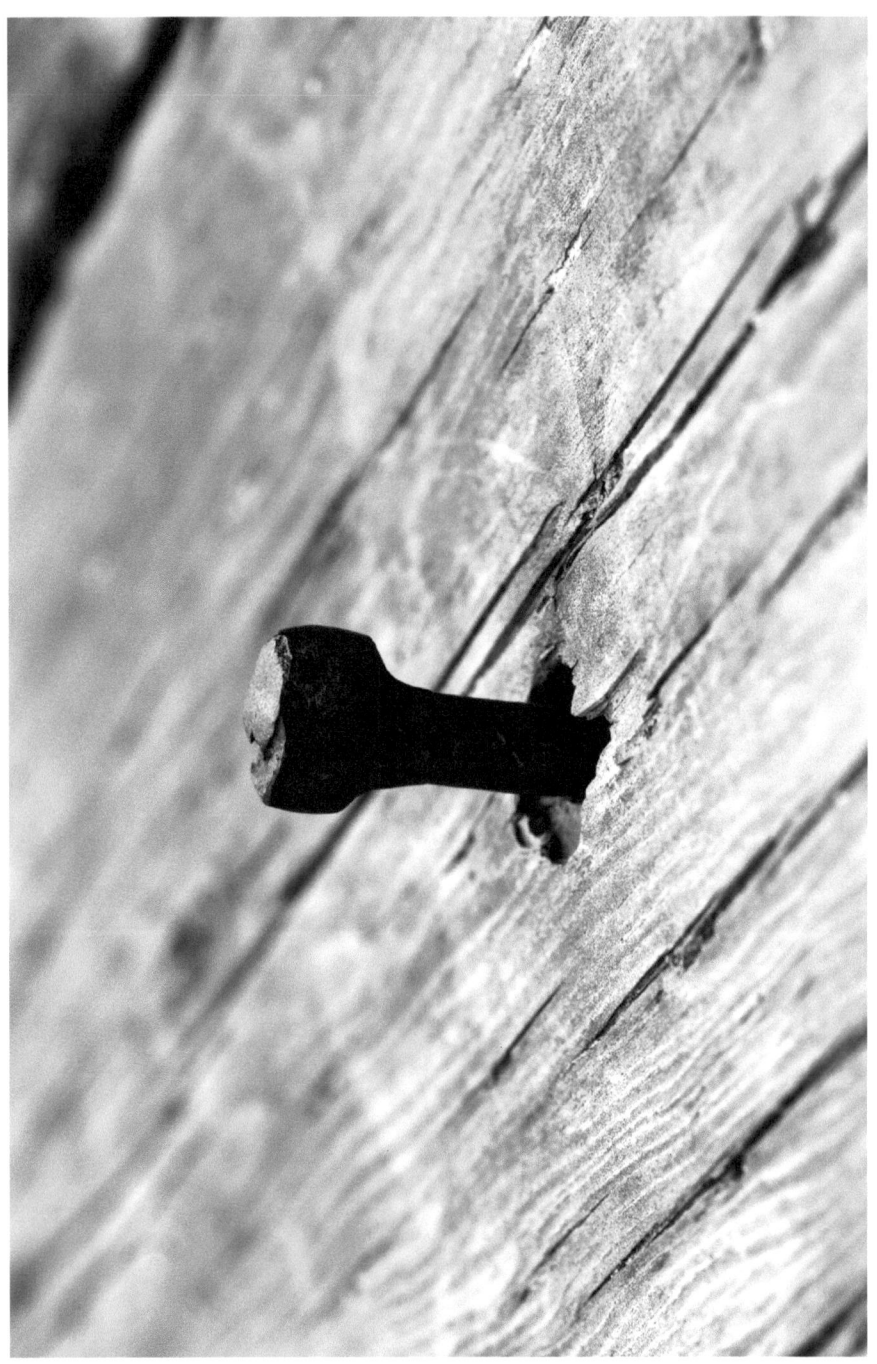

9024

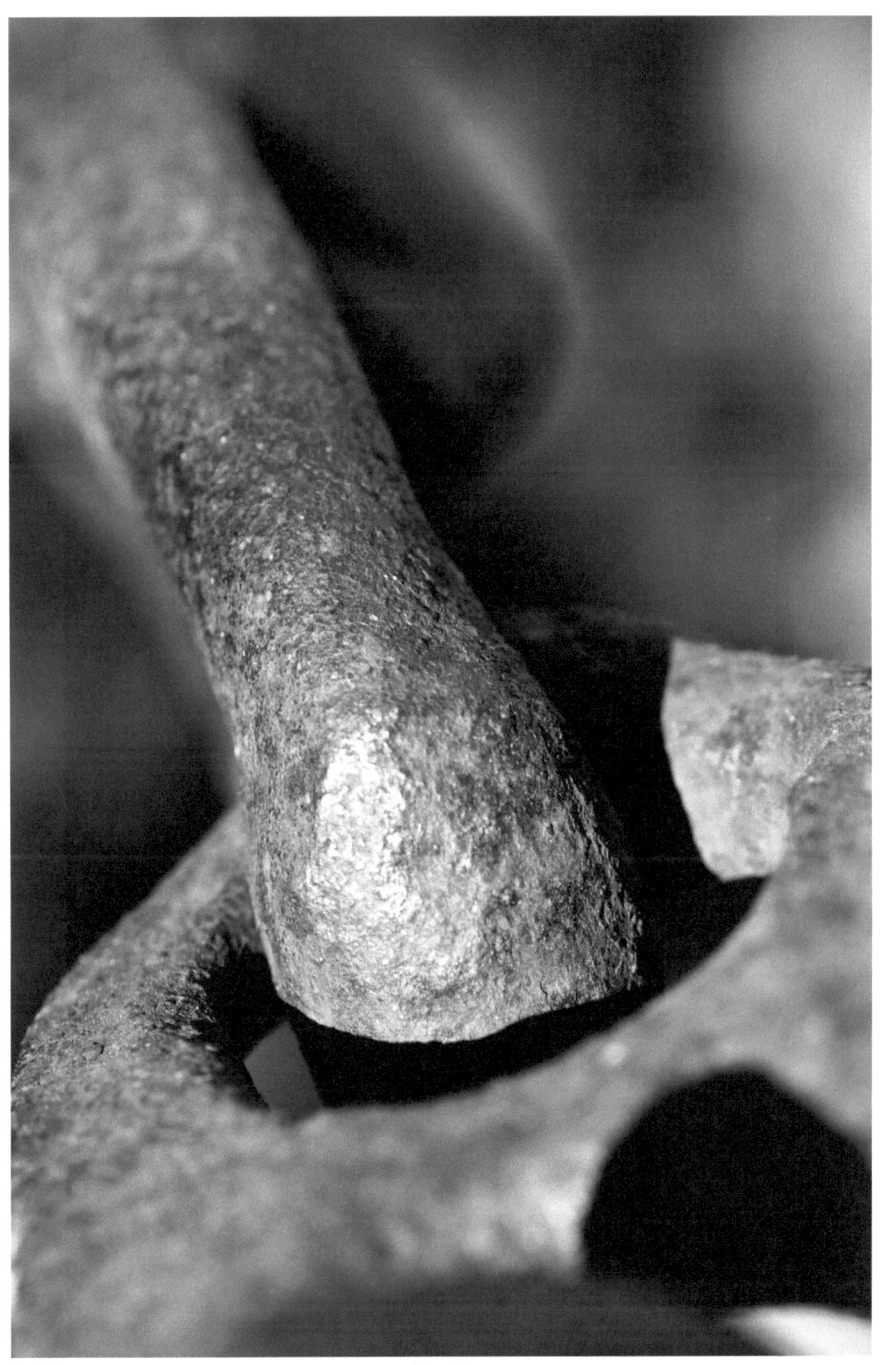

9353

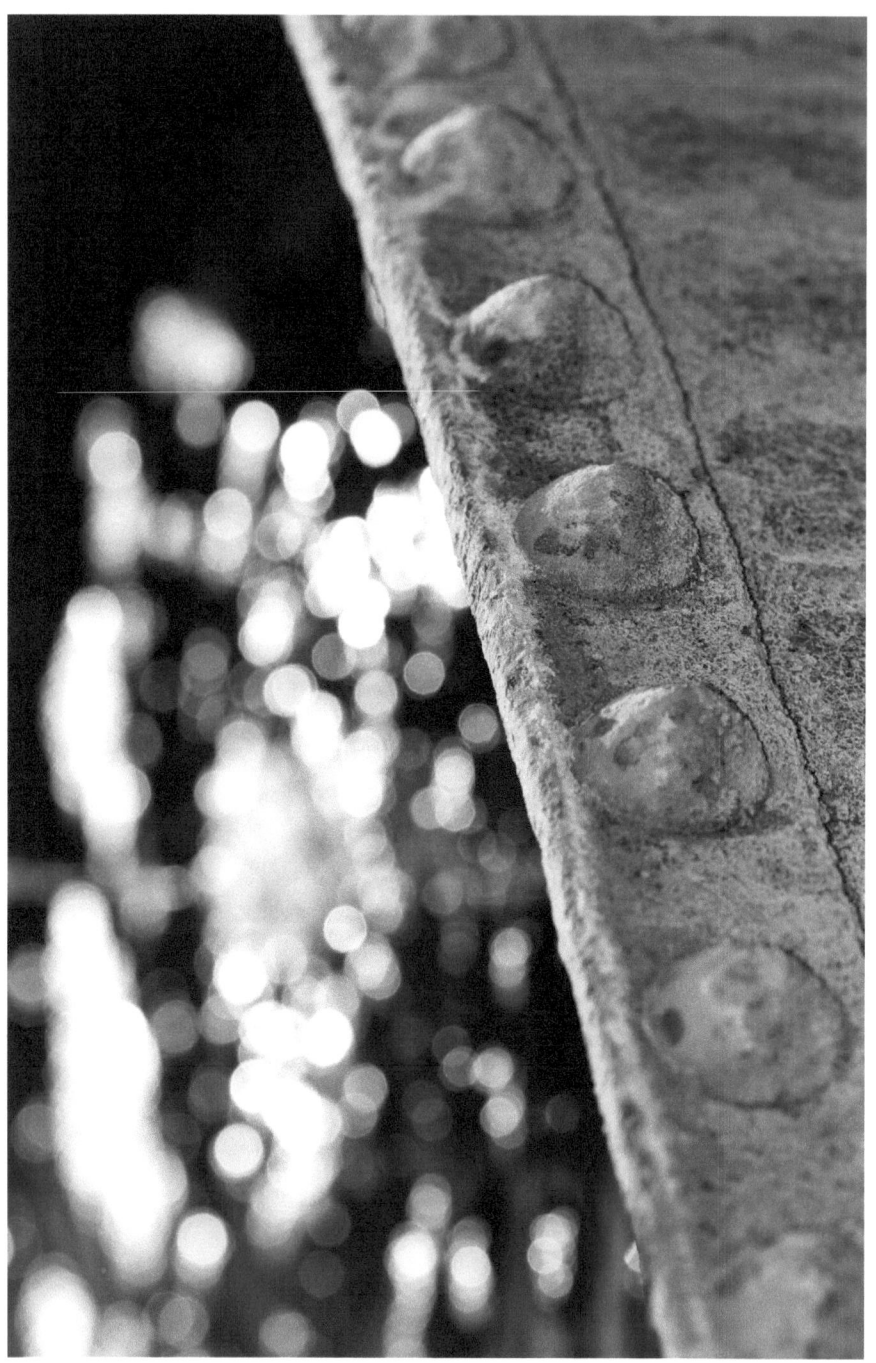

9430

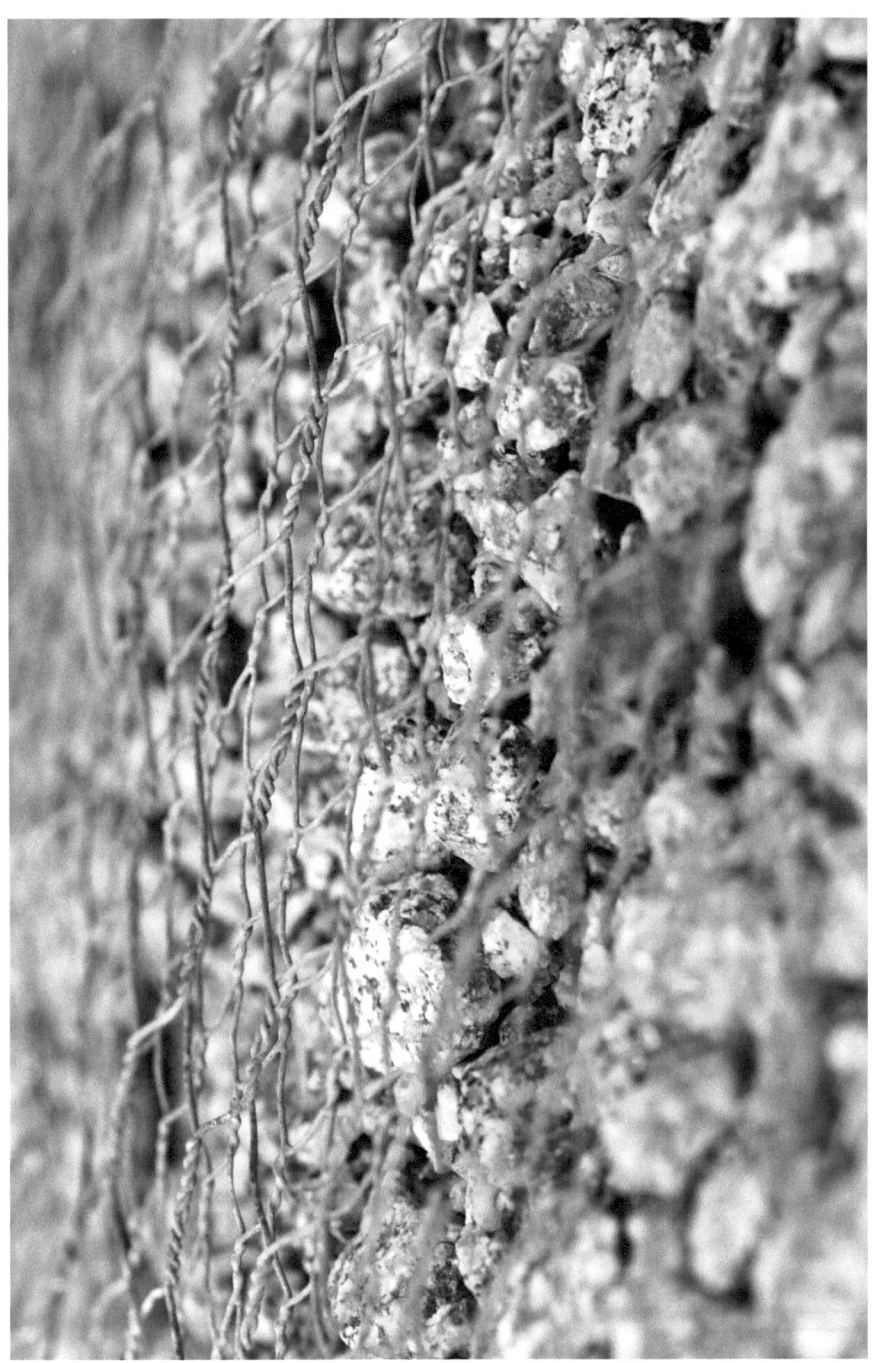

9970

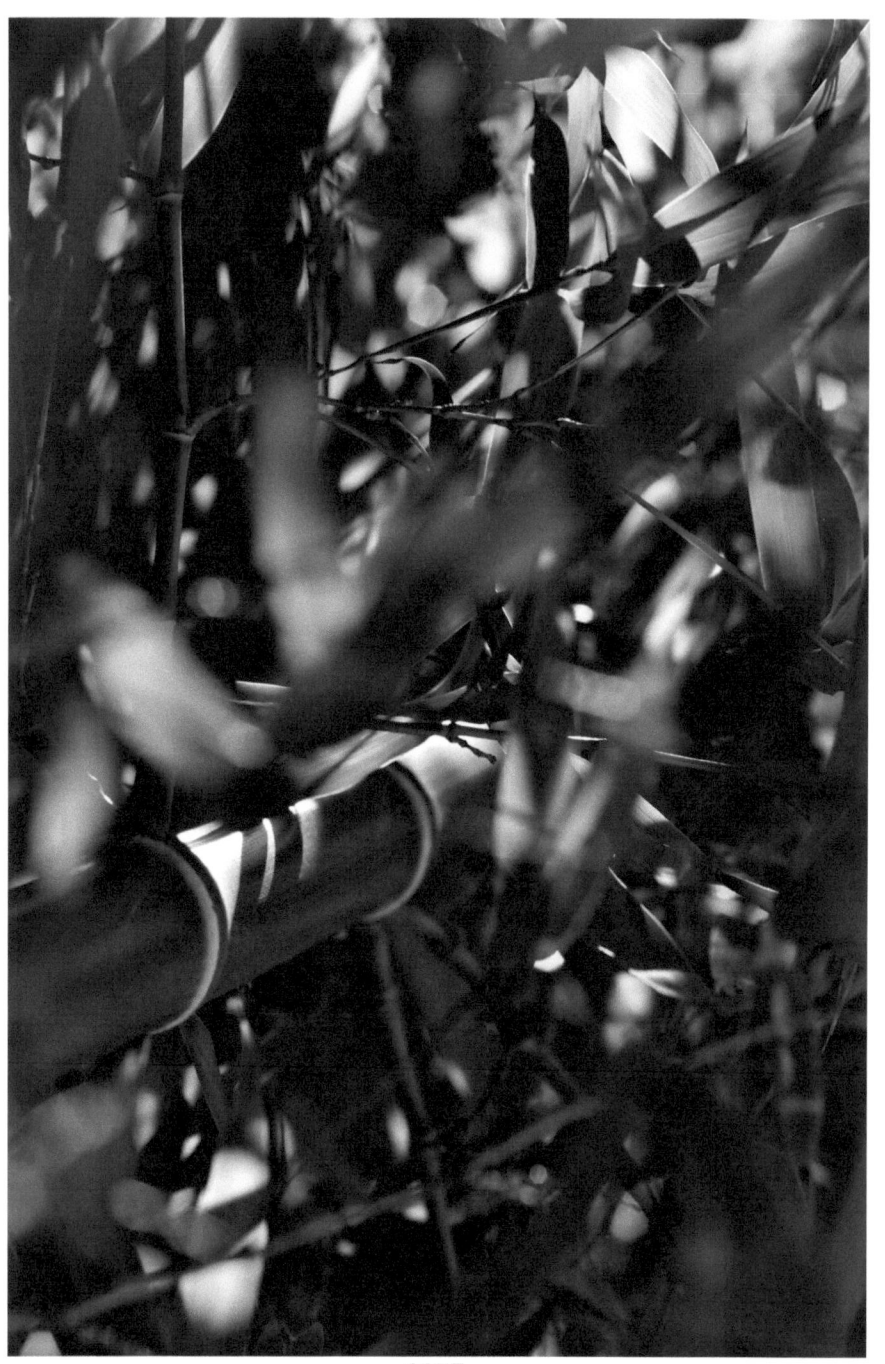

9975

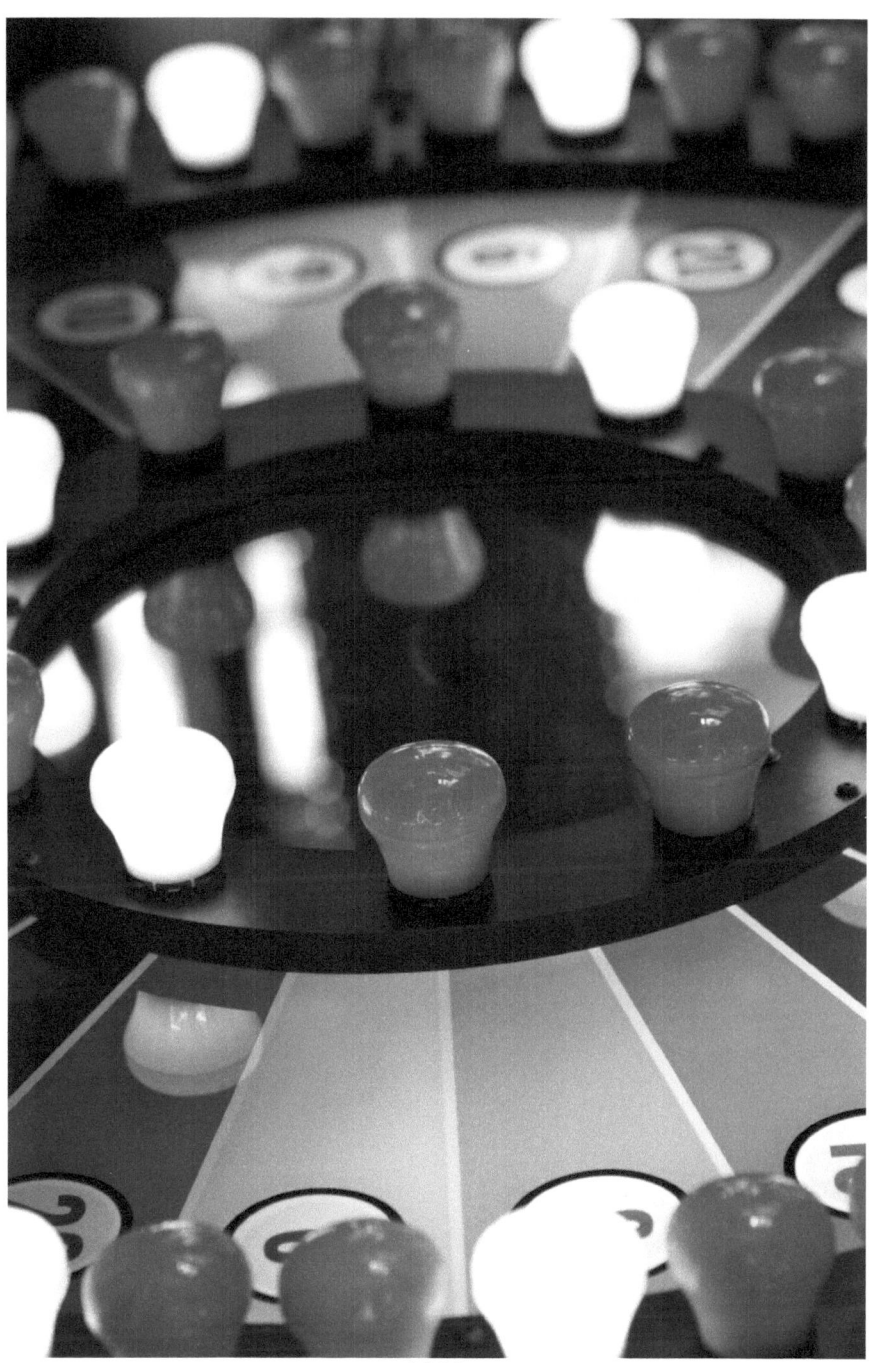

9980

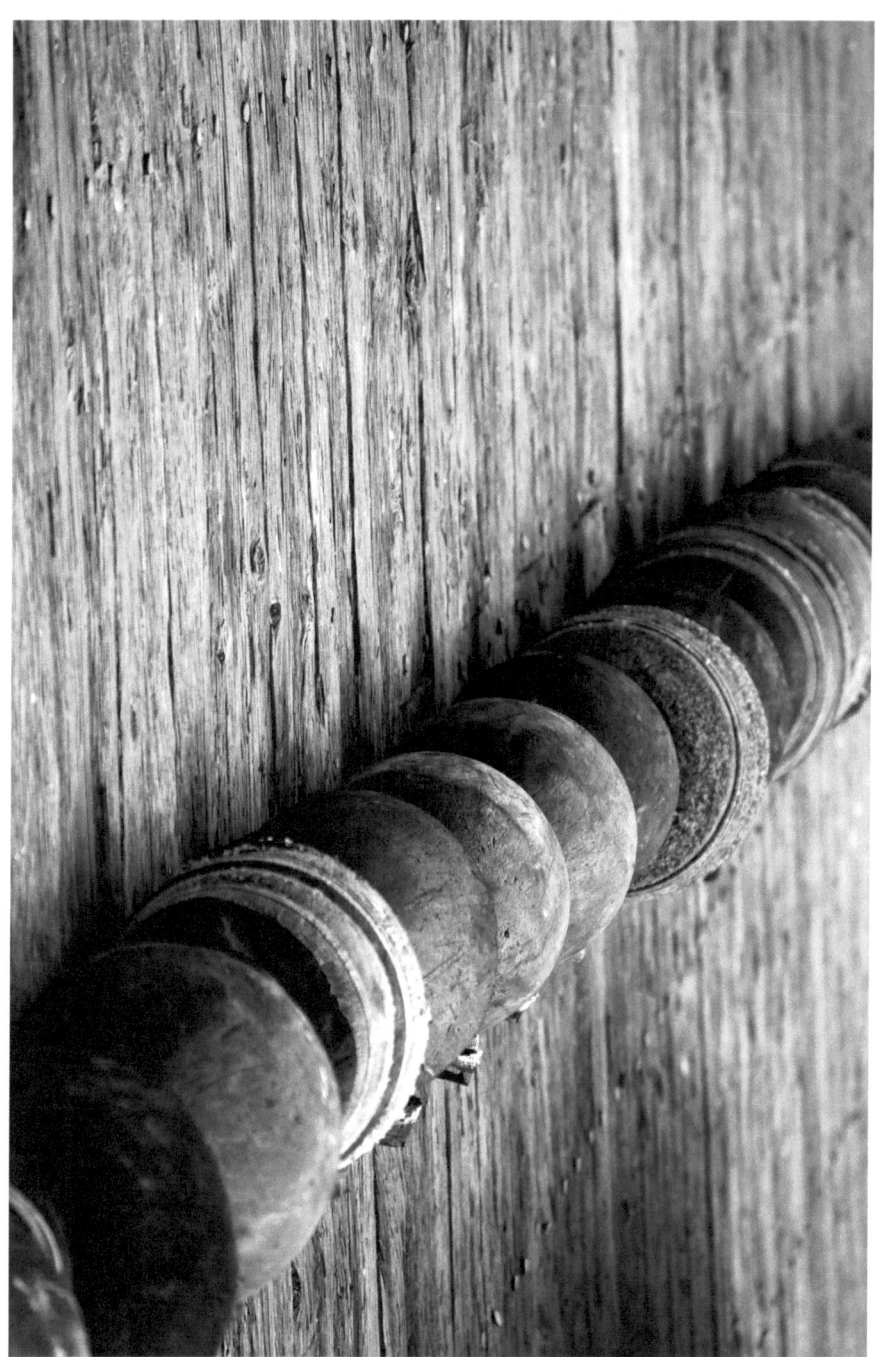

9998

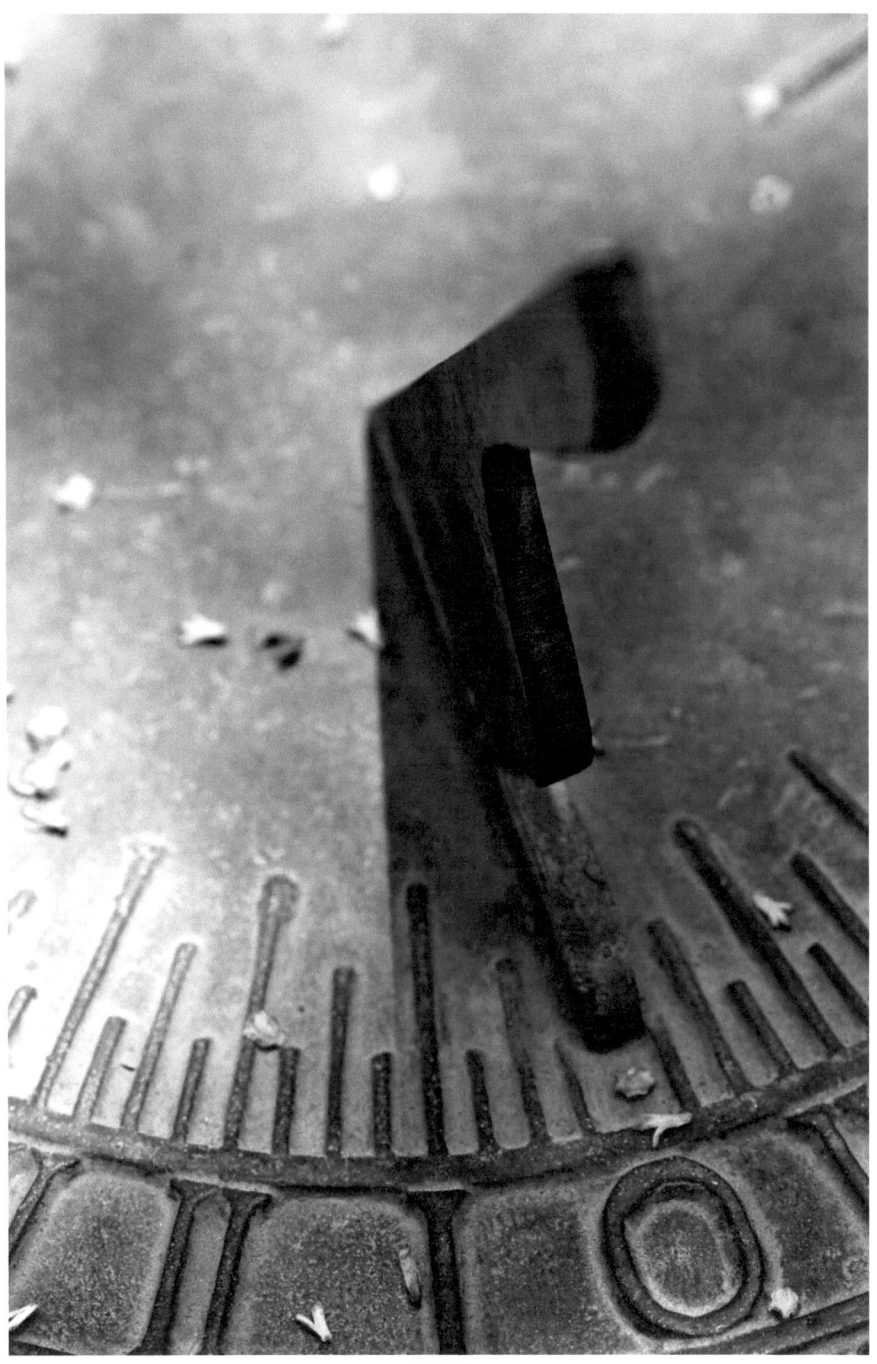

10002